The Wounds of Civil War by Thomas Lodge

Lively Set Forth in the True Tragedies of Marius and Scilla.

As it hath been publiquely plaide in London, by the Right Honourable the Lord High Admiral his Servants.

As can be easily understood presenting an exact chronicle of the facts in the life of a 16th Century playwright is often difficult. Thomas Lodge is no exception.

Thomas Lodge, born around 1558 in west Ham, was the second son of Sir Thomas Lodge, the Lord Mayor of London, and his third wife Anne.

Lodge was educated at Merchant Taylors' School and thence to Trinity College, Oxford; taking his BA in 1577 and his MA in 1581.

Lodge, disregarded his parents career wishes in order to take up literature. When the penitent Stephen Gosson published his Schoole of Abuse in 1579, Lodge responded with Defence of Poetry, Music and Stage Plays (1579 or 1580). His pamphlet was banned, but appears to have been circulated privately.

Already in 1580 Lodge had published a volume of poems entitled Scillaes Metamorphosis, Enterlaced with the Unfortunate Love of Glaucus, also more briefly known as Glaucus and Scilla.

Lodge seems to have married his first wife Joan in or shortly before 1583, when, "impressed with the uncertainty of human life", he made a will. That his family viewed his conduct at the time with disdain may be noted by the absence of his name from his father's will in 1583.

The marriage of Lodge and Joan produced a daughter, Mary. However, without an income from his family Lodge would have to provide it by other means.

The debate in pamphlets between Lodge and Gosson continued with Gosson's Playes Confuted in Five Actions; and Lodge retorting with his Alarum Against Usurers (1585)—a "tract for the times".

That same year, 1585, he produced his first tale written in prose and verse, The Delectable History of Forbonius and Prisceria.

Lodge appears to have been at sea on a number of long voyages. Usually these are described as 'freebooting voyages', an interchangeable term also used for piracy and plunder. Many nations endorsed these tactics and it seems fairly safe to suggest that these voyages were a source of revenue which would keep Joan and Mary with their heads above water. These long voyages also provided something else that Lodge would have been keen to gather and usefully use; time. During the expedition to Terceira and the Canaries (around 1586), to set aside the tedium of his voyage, Lodge composed his prose tale of Rosalynde, Euphues Golden Legacie, which, printed in 1590, would later be used by Shakespeare as the basis for As You Like It.

Before starting on his next voyage, this time to South America, Lodge published a historical romance, The History of Robert, Second Duke of Normandy, surnamed Robert the Devil; and he left behind him for publication Catharos Diogenes in his Singularity, a discourse on the immorality of Athens (London). Both appeared in 1591.

By now Lodge was on a voyage with Thomas Cavendish to Brazil and the Straits of Magellan and would only be able to return home in 1593. Whilst he was travelling another romance in the manner of Lyly, Euphues Shadow, the Battaile of the Sences, appeared in 1592.

At either end of this voyage Lodge appears to have worked on some dramas, most notably with Robert Greene.

It is thought that in 1590, together with Greene, he wrote A Looking Glass for London and England (published 1594). He had already written The Wounds of Civil War (produced perhaps as early as 1587, and published in 1594, and put on as a play reading at the Globe Theatre on 7 February 1606), a good second-rate piece in the half-chronicle fashion of its age.

His second historical romance, the Life and Death of William Longbeard (1593), was more successful than the first. Lodge also brought back with him from the new world voyage A Margarite of America (published 1596), a romance between a Peruvian prince and a daughter of the king of Muscovy interspersed with many lyrics.

The composition of Phillis, a volume and an early sonnet cycle sequence (an increasingly popular format in Elizabethan times), was published with the narrative poem, The Complaynte of Elsired, in 1593.

A Fig for Momus was published in 1595 and gained him the accolade of being the earliest English satirist. This work contains eclogues addressed to Daniel and others as well as an epistle addressed to Michael Drayton.

In the latter part of his life—possibly about 1596, when he published his Wits Miserie and the World's Madnesse, which is dated from Low Leyton in Essex, and the religious tract Prosopopeia (if, as seems probable, it was his), in which he repents of his "lewd lines" of other days—he became a Catholic and engaged in the practice of medicine, for which Wood says he qualified himself by a degree at Avignon, in France, in 1600. Two years later he received the degree of M.D. from Oxford University.

Early in 1606 he seems to have left England, to escape the persecution then directed against the Catholics; and a letter from him dated 1610 thanks the English ambassador in Paris for enabling him to return in safety.

At some point in his later life Lodge appears to have married again. This time to Jane Aldred, the widow of Solomon Aldred, at one time a Roman Catholic agent of Francis Walsingham in Rome.

From the early 1600's Lodge appears to have written or published sparingly. His later works include A Treatise of the Plague (1603) and two major translations—The Famous and Memorable Works of Josephus (1602) and The Works of Lucius Annaeus Seneca (1614), both of these went through several editions.

Obviously with his conversion to the Catholic faith life would have been difficult and most accounts agree that he withdrew from a literary life and instead concentrated on his work as a doctor. Over the years he was increasingly recognized as a distinguished physician and finally worked from Old Fish Street in the parish of St. Mary Magdalen.

Thomas Lodge died in London, most probably during an outbreak of the plague, in 1625.

Index of Contents

Dramatis Personae
In order of entrance
Sulpitius
Quintus Pompey
Junius Brutus
Lucretius
Lectorius.
Lucius Merula
Cynna
Caius Granius
Caius Marius
Mark Anthony
Scilla
Marius the younger, a Soldier of Scilla's.
Lepidus
Pausanius   }
Lucius Favorinus   } Magistrates of Minturnum
Cethegus, a Slave of Cynna
Octavius.
A young Citizen } of Rome
An old Citizen   }
A Jailor

Pedro, a Frenchman
Lucullus
Basillus
Arcathius   }
Aristion   } Captive Princes
Archelaus   }
Albinovanus, a Soldier of Marius'
Flaccus.
A Messenger.
Cornelia, wife of Scilla
Fulvia, her daughter
A Soldier of Marius'
A Clown, servant to Anthony
Three Soldiers of Marius'
A Captaine
Metellus
Carbo
Norbanus
Scipio
Publius Lentulus
Carinna, a Soldier of Marius the younger's
Tuditanus
Two Citizens of Praencste
Valerius Flaccus.
Curtall }
Poppey } Burghers
Genius.

Senators, Lictors, Captaines, Souldiers, an Ancient, Attendants on the magistrates of Minturnum, Roman Lords, Moors, Prisoners of divers nations, Citizens of Rome, Consular guard.

The Wounds of Civil War

The Most Lamentable and True Tragedies of Marius and Scilla

ACTUS PRIMA

SCENA PRIMA

Enter on the Capitoll **SULPITIUS TRIBUNE: CAIUS MARIUS: QUINTUS POMPEY CONSULL: LUNIUS BRUTUS: LUCRETIUS CAIUS GRANIUS LICTORIUS: LUCIUS MERULA** Jupiters Priest: and **CYNNA**: whom placed, and their **LICTORS** before them with their Rods and Axes, **SULPITIUS TRIBUNE** beginneth.

SULPITIUS TRIBUNE
Graue Senators and Fathers of this State,
Our strange protractions & unkind delays

wher waighty wars doth cal vs out to fight
Our factious wits to please aspiring Lords,
You see hath added powre vnto our foes,
And hazarded rich Phrigia and Bithinia,
With all our Asian Holds and Cities too:
Thus Scilla seeking to be Generall,
(Who is inuested in our Consuls Pall)
Hath forced murders in a quiet State:
The cause whereof euen Pompey may complaine,
Who seeking to aduance a climing friend,
Hath lost by death a sweete and curteous sonne.
Who now in Asia but Mithridates,
Laughs at these fond discentions I complaine?
While we in wrangling for a Generall,
Forsake our friends, forestall our forward warre,
And leaue our Legions full of dalliance,
Waighting our idle wills at Capua.
Fie Romaines, shall the glories of your names,
The wondrous beauty of this Capitoll,
Perish through Scillas insolence and pride,
As if that Rome were robd of true renowne,
And destitute of warlike Champions now?
Loe here the man, the rumor of whose fame,
Hath made Hiberia tremble and submit;
See Marius that in managing estate,
Through many cares and troubles he hath past,
And spent his youth, upon whose reuerend head
The milke-white pledge of wisedome sweetly spreds:
He sixe times Consul, fit for peace or warre,
Sits drooping here content to brooke disgrace,
Who glad to fight through follies of his foes
Sighs for your shame whilst you abide secure;
And I that see and should recure these wrongs,
Through Pompeys late vacation and delay,
Haue left to publish him for Generall,
That merites better titles farre than these:
But (Nobles) now the finall day is come,
When I your Tribune studying for renowne,
Pronounce and publish Marius Generall,
To leade our Legions against Mithridates,
And craue (graue Fathers) signes of your content,

QUINTUS POMPEY
Beleeue me Noble Romains, & graue Senators,
This strange election, and this new made Law,
Will witnes our vnstable gouernement,
And dispossesse Rome of her Emperie;
For although Marius be renownd in Armes,

Famous for prowesse, and graue in warlike drifts,
Yet may the sunne-shine of his former deeds
Nothing eclipse our Scillas dignity:
By lot and by election he was made,
Chiefe Generall against Mithridates,
And shall we then abridge him of that Rule;
'T were iniurie to Scilla and to Rome:
Nor would the height of his all daring minde,
Brooke to the death so vile and fowle disgrace.

LUNIUS BRUTUS

Why Pompey, as if the Senate had not powre
To appoint, dispose, & change their Generals:
Rome shall belike be bound to Scillas Rule,
Whose haughty pride and swelling thoughts puft up,
Foreshowes the reaching to prowd Tarquins state:
Is not his lingring to our Romaine losse
At Capua where he braues it out with feasts,
Made knowne thinke you unto the Senate here?
Yes Pompey, yes: and hereof are we sure
If Romaines State on Scillas pride should lie,
Romes Conquests would to Pontus Regions flie:
Therefore graue and renowned Senators,
(Pillers that beare and hold our Rule aloft,
You stately, true, and rich Piramides)
Descend into the depth of your estates,
Then shall you finde that Scilla is more fit,
To Rule in Rome domesticall affaires,
Then haue the Conquest of Bithinia,
Which if once got, heele but by death forgoe,
Therefore I say Marius our Generall.

LUCRETIUS

Lo thus we striue abroad to win renowne,
And naught regard at home our waning states;
Brutus I say the many braue exploits,
The warlike Acts that Scilla hath atchieude,
Showes him a souldier and a Romaine too,
Whose care is more for Country than himselfe:
Scilla nill brooke that in so many warres,
So hard aduentures and so strange extreames,
Hath borne the palme and prize of victory,
Thus with dishonor to give up his charge:
Scilla hath friends and souldiers at commaund,
That first will make the towres of Rome to shake,
And force the stately Capitoll to daunce,
Yer any robbe him of his just renowne:
Then we that through the Caspian shores haue runne,

And spread with ships the Orientall Sea,
At home shall make a murder of our friends,
And massaker our dearest Countrimen.

LICTOR
The powre of Scilla nought will vaile gainst Rome,
And let me die Lucretius ere I see,
Our Senate dread for any priuate man,
Therefore Renownd Sulpitius send for Scilla backe,
Let Marius leade our men in Asia.

MERULA
The Law, the Senate wholy doth affirme,
Let Marius lead our men in Asia.

CYNNA
Cynna affirmes the Senates Censure iust,
And saith let Marius leade the Legions forth.

GRANIUS
Honor and victory follow Marius steps,
For him doth Granius wish to fight for Rome.

SULPITIUS
Why then you sage and auncient Syres of Rome,
Sulpitius here againe doth publish forth,
That Marius by the Senate here is made,
Chiefe Generall to lead the Legions out,
Against Mithridates and his Competitors,
Now victory for honor of Rome follow Marius.
Here let Marius rowse him selfe.

MARIUS
Sage and imperiall Senators of Rome,
Not without good aduisement haue you seene,
Old Marius silent during your discourse:
Yet not for that he feard to pleade his cause,
Or raise his honor troden downe by age,
But that his words should not allure his friends,
To stand on stricter tearmes for his behoofe:
Sixe times the Senate by election hath,
Made Marius Consul ouer warlike Rome,
And in that space nor Rome nor all the world,
Could euer say that Marius was untrue,
These siluer haires that hang upon my face,
Are witnesses of my unfained zeale,
The Cymbrians that yer-while inuaded France,
And held the Romaïne Empire in disdaine,

Lay all confounded under Marius sword,
Fierce Scipio the myrrour once of Rome,
whose losse as yet my inward soule bewailes,
Being askt who should succeede and beare his Rule,
Even this (quod he) shall Scipios armour beare,
And therewithall clapt me upon the backe:
If then graue Lords, my former passed youth,
was spent in bringing Honors into Rome,
Let then my age and latter date of yeares,
Be sealed up for honor unto Rome.

[Here enter **SCILLA** with **CAPTAINES** and **SOULDIERS**.

SULPITIUS
Scilla, what means these Arms and warlike troops
These glorious Ensignes and these fierce Allarms,
Tis prowdly done to braue the Capitoll.

SCILLA
These Armes Sulpitius are not borne for hate,
But maintenance of my confirmed state:
I come to Rome with no seditious thoughts,
Except I finde too froward iniuries.

SULPITIUS
But wisedome would you did forbeare,
To yeeld these flight suspitions of contempt,
where as this Senate studieth high affaires.

SCILLA
what serious matters haue these Lords in hand?

SULPITIUS
The Senators with full decree appoint,
Old Marius for their Captaine Generall,
To leade thy Legions into Asia,
And fight against the fierce Mithridates.

SCILLA
To Marius? lolly stuffe: why then I see,
Your Lordships meane to make a babe of me.

LUNIUS BRUTUS
Tis true Scilla the Senate hath agreed,
That Marius shall those bands and Legions beare,
which you now hold against Mithridates.

SCILLA

Marius shal lead them then, if Scilla said not no,
And I shall bea Consuls shadow then,
Trustles Senators and ingratefull Romaines,
For all the Honors I haue done to Rome,
For all the spoiles I brought within her walles,
Thereby for to enrich and raise her pride,
Repay you me with this ingratitude:
You know unkinde, that Scillas wounded Helme,
Was nere hung up or once distaind with rust:
The Marcians that before me fell amaine,
And like to winter haile on every side,
Unto the City Nuba I pursude,
And for your sakes were thirty thousand slaine:
The Hippinians and the samnits scilla brought,
As Tributaries unto famous Rome:
I, where did scilla euer draw his sword,
Or lift his warlike hand above his head
For Romaines cause but he was Conquerour:
And now (unthankeful) seeke you to disgrade,
And teare the plumes that scillas sword hath wonne.
Marius I tell thee scilla is the man,
Disdaines to stoope or vaile his pride to thee;
Marius I say thou maist nor shalt not haue,
The charge that unto scilla doth belong,
Unlesse thy sword could teare it from my hart,
Which in a thousand folds impalls the same.

MARIUS
And scilla hereof be thou full assurde,
The honor whereto mine undaunted minde,
And this graue senate hath enhaunsed me,
Thou nor thy followers shall derogate,
The spence of yeares that Marius hath ore-past,
Inforraine broyles and ciuil mutenies,
Hath taught him this, that one unbrideled foe,
My former fortunes never shall oregoe.

SCILLA
Marius, I smile at these thy foolish words,
And credit me should laugh outright I feare,
If that I knew not how thy froward age,
Doth make thy sence as feeble as thy ioynts.

MARIUS
Scilla, Scilla, Marius yeeres hath taught
Him how to plucke so proud a yonkers plumes,
And know these haires that dangle downe my face,
In brightnes like the siluer Rodope:

Shall add so haughtie courage to my minde,
And rest such percing obiects gainst thine eies,
That maskt in follie, age shall force thee stoope.

SCILLA

And by my hand I sweare ere thou shalt mase mee so,
My soule shall perish but Ile haue thy bearde,
Say graue Senators shall Scilla be your Generall.

SULPITIUS

No the Senate, I and Rome her selfe agrees,
Ther's none but Marius shall be Generall.
Therefore Scilla these daring tearmes unfit,
Beseeme not thee before the Capitoll.

SCILLA

Beseeme not me? Senators aduise you,
Scilla hath vowd whose vowes the heauens recorde,
Whose othes hath pierst and searcht the deepest vast,
I and whose protestations raigne on earth:
This Capitoll wherein your glories shine,
Was nere so prest and throng de with scarlet gownes,
As Rome shall be with heapes of slaughtred soules
Before that Scilla yeeld his titles up,
Ile mate hir streets that peere into the clouds,
Burnisht with gold and Iuorie pillors faire,
Shining with Iasper, Iet, and Ebonie,
All like the pallace of the morning sunne,
To swim within a sea of purple blood
Before I loose the name of Generall.

MARIUS

These threats against thy country and these Lords.
Scilla proceeds from forth a Traitorshart,
Whose head I trust to see aduanced up
On highest top of all this Capitoll:
As earst was manie of thy progenie,
Before thou vaunt thy victories in Rome.

SCILLA

Graybeard, if so thy hart and tongue agree,
Draw forth thy Legions and thy men at armes,
Reare up thy standerd and thy steeled Crest,
And meete with Scilla in the fields of Mars,
And trie whose fortune makes him Generall.

MARIUS

I take thy word: Marius will meet thee there,

And proue thee Scilla a Traitor vnto Rome,
And all that march vnder thy traiterous wings,
Therefore they that loue the Senate and Marius
Now follow him.

SCILLA
And all that loue Scilla come downe to him,
For the rest let them follow Marius
And the Diuel himselfe be their Captaine.

[Here let the Senate rise and cast away their Gownes, hauing their swords by their sides: Exit **MARIUS**
and with him **SULPITIUS: LUNIUS BRUTUS: LECTORIUS**.

POMPEY
Scilla, I come to thee,

LUCRETIUS
Scilla, Lucretius will die with thee,

SCILLA
Thankes my Noble Lords of Rome.

[Here let them goe downe and **SCILLA** offers to goe forth and **MARK ANTHONY** calls him backe,

MARK ANTHONY
Stay Scilla, heare Anthony breath forth,
The pleading plaints of sad declining Rome.

SCILLA
Anthony, thou knowst thy hony words doo pierce,
And moue the minde of Scilla to remorse:
Yet neither words nor pleadings now must serue,
When as mine honor calls me forth to fight,
Therefore sweete Anthony be short for Scillas hast.

MARK ANTHONY
For Scillas hast, O whither wilt thou flie?
Tell me my Scilla what dost thou take in hand?
What warres are these thou stirrest vp in Rome?
What fire is this is kindled by thy wrath!
A fire that must be quencht by Romaines blood,
A warre that will confound our Emperie,
And last an Act of fowle impietie.
Brute beasts nill breake the mutuall law of loue,
And birds affection will not violate,
The senceles trees haue concord mongst themselues,
And stones agree in linkes of amitie,
If they my Scilla brooke not to haue iarre,

What then are men that gainst themselues doo warres
Thoult say my Scilla honor stures thee up:
Ist honor to infringe the lawes of Rome?
Thoult say perhaps the titles thou hast wonne,
It were dishonor for thee to forgoe:
O, is there any height aboue the highe,
Or any better than the best of all?
Art thou not Consul? Art thou not Lord of Rome?
What greater Tytles should our Scilla haue?
But thou wilt hence, thou wilt fight with Marius
The man, the Senate, I and Rome hath chose.
Thinke this before, thou neuer liftst aloft,
And lettest fall thy warlike hand adowne,
But thou dost raze and wound thy Citie Rome:
And looke how many slaughtred soules he slaine,
Under thy Ensignes, and thy conquering Launce,
so many murders makest thou of thy selfe.

SCILLA

Inough my Anthony, for thy honied tongue
Washt in a sirrop of sweete Conseruatiues,
Driueth confused thoughts through scillas minde,
Therfore suffize thee, I may nor will not heare,
so farewell Anthony, honor calls me hence,
scilla will fight for glorie and for Rome.

[Exit **SCILLA** and his followers.

MERULA

See Noble Anthony the trustles state of rule,
The stayles hold of matchles soueraignetie,
Now fortune beareth Rome into the Clowds,
To throw her downe into the lowest hells,
For they that spread her glory through the world,
Are they that tease her prowd triumphant plumes:
The hart-burning pride of prowd Tarquinius,
Rooted from Rome the sway of kingly mace,
And now this discord newly set abroach,
Shall ease our Consuls and our Senates downe.

MARK ANTHONY

Unhappy Rome and Romaines thrise accurst,
That oft with triumphs sild your Citie walls,
With kings and conquering Rulers of the world,
Now to eclipse in top of all thy pride,
Through ciuill discords and domesticke broiles:
O Romaines weepe the teares of sad lament,
And rent your sacred Robes at this exchange,

For Fortune makes our Rome a banding ball,
Tost from her hand to take the greater fall.

GRANIUS
O whence proceeds these fowle ambitious thoughts,
That fires mens harts and makes them thirst for Rule:
Hath soueraignty so much be witcht the minds
Of Romaines: that their former busied cares
Which erst did tire in seeking Cities good,
Must now be changd to ruine of her walls?
Must they that heard her stately Temples up,
Deface the sacred places of their Gods?
Then may we waile and wring our wretched hands,
Sith both our Gods, our temples and our walls,
Ambition makes fell fortunes spightfull thralls.

[Exeunt all.

[A great Alarum: let young **MARIUS** chase **POMPEY** over the stage, and old **MARIUS** chase
LUCRETIUS Then let enter three or foure **SOULDIERS** and his Auntient with his cullors, and **SCILLA** after
them with his hat in his hand, they offer to flie away.

SCILLA
Why whither flie you Romaines,
What mischiefe makes this flight?
Stay good my friends, stay dearest Countrimen.

1ˢᵗ SOULDIER
Stay let vs heare what our Lord Scilla saith.

SCILLA
What wil you leaue your chieftains Romains then?
And loose your Honors in the gates of Rome?
What shall our Country see, and Scilla rue,
These Coward thoughts so fixt and firmd in you?
What are you come from Capua to proclaime,
Your harties treasons in this happy towne?
What will you stand and gaze with shameles looks,
Whilst Marius butchering knife assailes our throat's?
Are you the men, the hopes, the staires of state?
Are you the souldiers prest for Asia?
Are you the wondered Legions of the world,
And will you flie these shadows of resist?
Well Romaines I will perish through your pride,
That thought by you to haue returnd in pompe.
And at the least your Generall shall proue,
Euen in his death your treasons and his loue.
Lo this the wreath that shall my body binde,

Whilst Scilla sleepes with honor in the field:
And I alone within these cullors shut,
Will blush your dastard follies in my death,
So farewell hartles souldiers and untrue,
That leaue your Scilla who hath loued you.

[Exit.

1st SOULDIER

Why fellow souldiers shall we flie the field,
And carelesly forsake our Generall?
What shall our vowes conclude with no auaile?
First die sweete friends, and shed your purple blood,
Before you lose the man that wills you good.
Then to it braue Italians out of hand:
Scilla we come with fierce and deadly blowes,
To venge thy wrongs and vanquish all thy toes.

[Exeunt to the Alarum.

ACTUS SECONDA

SCENA PRIMA

Appian solus.

Enter **SCILLA** triumphant, **LUCRETIUS**, **POMPEY**, with **SOULDIER**.

SCILLA

You Romaine souldiers, fellow mates in Armes,
The blind fold Mistris of incertaine chaunce,
Hath turnd these traiterous climers from the top,
And seated Scilla in the chiefest place.
The place beseeming Scilla and his minde,
For were the throne where matchles glorie sits,
Empald with furies threatning blood and death,
Begirt with famine and those fatall feares
That dwell below amidst the dreadfull vast:
Tut Scillaes sparkling eyes should dim with cleere
The burning brands of their consuming light,
And master fancie with a forward minde,
And maske repining feare with awfull power.
For men of baser mettall and conceipt
Cannot conceiue the beautie of my thought.
I crowned with a wreath of warlike state,
Imagine thoughts more greater than a crowne,

And yet befitting well a Romane minde.
Then gentle ministers of all my hopes,
That with your swords made way unto my wish,
Hearken the frutes of your couragious fight,
In spite of all these Romane Bafilisks,
That seeke to quell vs with their currish lookes,
We will to Pontus weele haue gold my harts,
Those orientall pearles shall decke our browes:
And you my gentle friends, you Romane peeres,
Kinde Pompey worthie of a Consulls name.
You shall abide the father of the state,
Whilst these braue lads Lucretius and I,
In spight of all these brauling Senators,
Will, shall, and dare attempt on Asia,
And driue Mithridates from out his doores.

POMPEY
I Scilla, these are words of mickle worth,
Fit for the master of so great a minde:
Now Rome must stoop, for Marius and his frends
Haue left their armes, and trust unto their heeles.

SCILLA
But Pompey, if our Spanish Iennets feete
Haue learnt to poast it of their mother winde,
I hope to nip upon the gray beards heeles,
Till I haue cropt his shoulders from his head.
As for his sonne, the proud aspiring boy,
His beardlesse face and wanton smiling browes,
Shall (if I catch him) decke yond Capitoll:
The father, sonne, the frends, and souldiers all,
That fawne on Marius, shall with furie fall.

LUCRETIUS
And what euent shall all these troubles bring?

SCILLA
This: Scilla in fortune will exceed a king.
But frends and souldiers, with dispersed bands
Goe seeke out Marius fond confederates:
some poast along those unfrequented paths,
That trackt by nookes unto the neighbring sea:
Murther me Marius, and maintaine my life.
And that his fauorites in Rome may learne
The difference betwixt my fawne and frowne,
Go cut them short, & shed their hatefull blood,

[Exit **SOULDIERS**.

To quench these furies of my froward mood.

LUCRETIUS
Loe scilla where our senators approach,
Perhaps to gratulate thy good successe.

[Enter **MARK ANTHONY, GRANIUS, LEPIDUS.**

SCILLA
I that perhaps was fitly placed there:
But my Lucretius, these are cunning Lords,
Whose tongues are tipt with honnie to deceiue:
As for their hearts, if outward eyes may see them,
The diuell scarce with mischiefe might agree them.

LEPIDUS
Good fortune to our Consull, worthy scilla.

SCILLA
And why not Generall against the king of Pontus?

GRANIUS
And generall against the king of Pontus.

SCILLA
Sirrha, your words are good, your thoughts are ill,
Each milke white haire amidst this mincing beard,
Compard with milions of thy trecherous thoughts,
Would change their hiew through vigor of thy hate.
But did not pitie make my furie thrall,
This sword should finish hate, thy life and all.
I pre thee Granius, how doth Marius?

GRANIUS
As he that bydes a thrall to thee and fate,
Liuing in hope as I and others doo,
To catch good fortune, and to crosse thee too.

SCILLA
Both blunt and bold but too much Mother wit;
To play with fier where furie streames about,
Curtall your tale fond man cut of the rest:
But here I will dissemble for the best.

GRANIUS
Scilla my yeares hath taught me to discerne,
Betwixt ambitious pride and Princely zeale,

And from thy youth these Peeres of Rome have markt,
A rash reuenging hammer in thy braine,
Thy tongue adornde with flowing eloquence,
And yet I see imprinted in thy browes,
A fortunate but froward gouernaunce.
And though thy riuall Marius mated late,
By backward working of his wretched fate
Is falne, yet Scilla marke what I haue seene
Euen here in Rome the Fencer Spectacus,
Hath bin as fortunate as thou thy selfe:
But when that Crassus sword assayed his crest,
The feare of death did make him droope for woe.

SCILLA
You saw in Rome this brawling fencer die,
When Spectacus by Crassus was subdewd:
Why so, but sir I hope you will applie,
And say like Spectacus that I shall die?
Thus peeuish eld discoursing by a fire,
Amidst their cups will prate how men aspire:
Is this the greeting Romanes that you giue,
Unto the Patron of your Monarchie?
Lucretius shall I play a prettie iest.

LUCRETIUS
What Scilla will, what Romane dare withstand?

SCILLA
A briefe and pleasing answere by my head,
Why tell me Granius dost thou talke in sport?

GRANIUS
No Scilla my discourse is resolute,
Not coynd to please thy fond and cursed thoughts:
For were my tongue betraide with pleasing words,
To feed the humors of thy haughty mind:
I rather wish the rot should roote it out.

SCILLA
The brauest brawler that I euer heard,
But souldiers since I see he is opprest
With crooked choller, and our Artists teach,
That fretting blood will presse through opened veines,
Let him that hath the keenest sword arrest,
The gray-beard and cut off his head in iest.
Souldiers lay hands on Granius.

GRANIUS

Is this the guerdon then of good aduise?

SCILLA
No but the meanes to make fond men more wise,
Tut I haue wit, and carry warlike tooles,
To charme the scolding prate of wanton fooles,
Tell me of Fencers and a tale of Fate?
No, scilla thinkes of nothing but a state.

GRANIUS
Why scilla I am armd the worst to trie.

SCILLA
I pray thee then Lucretius let him die.

[Exeunt with **GRANIUS**.

Beshrow me Lords but in this iolly vame,
Twere pitty but the prating foole were slaine:
I feare me Pluto will be wroth with me,
For to detaine so graue a man as he.

MARK ANTHONY
But seeke not scilla in this quiet state,
To worke reuenge upon an aged man,
A senator, a soueraigne of this towne.

SCILLA
The more the Cedar climes the sooner downe
And did I thinke the prowdest man in Rome,
Would winch at that which I haue wrought or done,
I would and can controwle his insolence.
Why senators, is this the true reward,
Wherewith you answere Princes for their paine,
As when this sword hath made our Citie free,
A brauing mate should thus distemper mee?
But Lepidus and fellow senators,
I am resolude and will not brooke your taunts,
Who wrongeth scilla, let him looke for stripes.

MARK ANTHONY
I but the milder passions show the man
For as the leafe doth beautifie the tree,
The pleasant flowres bedecke the painted spring,
Euen so in men of greatest reach and powre,
A milde and piteous thought augments renowne;
Old Anthony did neuer see my Lord,
A swelling showre that did continue long,

A climing towre that did not tast the wind,
A wrathfull man not wasted with repent,
I speake of loue my Scilla, and of ioy
To see how fortune lends a pleasant gale,
Unto the spreading sailes of thy desires:
And louing thee must counsaile thee withall,
For as by cutting fruitfull vines increase,
So faithfull counsailes workes a Princes peace.

SCILLA
Thou hony talking father speake thy minde.

MARK ANTHONY
My Scilla scarce those teares are dried up,
That Romaine Matrons wept to see this warre:
Along the holy streets the hideous grones,
Of murthered men infect the weeping aire:
Thy foes are fled not ouertaken yet,
And doubtfull is the hazard of this warre:
Yea doubtfull is the hazard of this warre,
For now our Legions draw their wastfull swords,
To murther whom? Euen Romaine Citizens.
To conquer whom? Euen Romaine Citizens.
Then if that Scilla loue these Citizens,
If care of Rome, if threat of forraine foes,
If fruitfull counsailes of thy forward friends
May take effect, goe fortunate and driue,
The king of Pontus out of Asia,
Least while we dreame on ciuill mutenies,
Our wary foes assaile our Citie walls.

POMPEY
My long concealed thoughts Mark Anthony,
Must seeke discouerie through thy pliant words:
Beleeue me Scilla ciuill mutenies,
Must not obscure thy glories and our names:
Then sith that factious Marius is supprest,
Goe spread thy colours midst the Asian fields,
Meane while my selfe will watch this Cities weale.

SCILLA
Pompey I know thy loue, I marke thy words,
And Anthony thou hast a pleasing vaine,
But senators I hammer in my head,
With euery thought of honor some reuenge:

[Enter **LUCRETIUS** with the head.

Speake what shall Scilla be your Generall?

LEPIDUS
We doo decree that Scilla shall be Generall:

SCILLA
And wish you Scillas weale and honour too?

MARK ANTHONY
We wish both Scillas weale and honor too

SCILLA
Then take away the scandall of this state,
Banish the name of Tribune out of towne,
Proclaime false Marius and his other friends.
Foe men and traitors to the state of Rome,
And I will wend and worke so much by force,
As I will master false Mithridates,

LEPIDUS
The name of Tribune hath continued long.

SCILLA
So shall not Lepidus if he withstand me.
Sirra you see the head of Granius,
Watch you his hap unlesse you change your words,
Pompey now please me Pompey graunt my sute.

POMPEY
Lictors proclaime this our undanted doome,
we will that Marius and his wretched sonnes,
His friends Sulpitius, Claudius and the rest
Beheld for traytors, and acquit the men
That shall endanger there unluckie lines,
And henceforth Tribunes name and state shall cease,
Graue Senators how like you this decree?

LEPIDUS
Euen as our Consulls wish, so let it be.

SCILLA
Then Lepidus all friends in faith for me,
So leaue I Rome to Pompey and my friends,
Resolud to manage those our Asian warres,
Frolike braue Souldiers wee must foote it now,
Lucretius you shall bide the brunt with me,
Pompey farewell, and farewell Lepidus.
Mark Anthony I leaue thee to thy books,

Study for Rome and Scillas Royaltie.
But by my sword I wrong this graybeards head,
Goe sirra place it on the Capitoll:
Aiust promotion fit for scillaes foe.
Lordings farewell, come souldiers let us goe.

[Exit.

POMPEY
Scilla farewell and happy be thy chaunce,
Whose warre both Rome and Romaines must a duaunce.

[Exeunt **SENATORS**.

[Enter the **MAGISTRATES** of Minturnum with **MARIUS** very melancholie, **LUCIUS FAVORINUS**,
PAUSANIUS with some attendants.

PAUSANIUS
My Lord the course of your unstaied fate,
Made weake through that your late unhappie fight,
Withdrawes our wills that faine would worke your weale:
For long experience and the change of times,
The innocent suppressions of the iust
In leaning to forsaken mens reliefe,
Doth make vs feare lest our unhappie towne,
should perish through the angrie Romaines sword.

MARIUS
Lords of Minturnum when I shapd my course,
To flie the danger of pursuing death,
I left my friends, and all alone attaind
(In hope of succors) to this little towne,
Relying on your curtesies and truth.
What foolish feare doth then amaze you thus?

FAVORINUS
O Marius, thou thy self, thy sonne, thy friends,
Are banished and exiles out of Rome,
Proclaimd for traitors, rest of your estates,
Adiudgde to death with certaine warrantize.
should then so small a towne my Lord as this,
Hazard their fortunes to supplie your wants?

MARIUS
Why Citizens, and what is Marius?
I tell you not so base as to dispaire,
Yea able to withstand ingratitudes.
Tell me of foolish lawes decreede at Rome,

To please the angrie humors of my foe:
Beleeue me Lords I know and am assurde,
That magnanimitie can neuer feare,
And fortitude so conquer silly fate,
As scilla when he hopes to haue my head,
May hap ere long on sodaine lose his owne.

PAUSANIUS
A hope beseeming Marius, but I feare,
Too strange to haue a short and good euent.

MARIUS
Why sir Pausanius haue not you beheld,
Campania plaines fulfild with greater foes,
Than is that wanton milke-sop natures scorne.
Base minded men to liue in perfect hope,
Whose thoughts are shut within your cottage eyes,
Refuse not Marius that must fauour you:
For these are parts of unaduised men,
With present feare to lose a perfect friend,
That can, will, may controwle, commaund, subdue,
That brauing boy that thus bewitcheth you.

FAVORINUS
How gladly would we succour you my Lord,
But that we feare.

MARIUS
What? the Moone-shine in the water.
Thou wretched stepdame of my fickle state,
Are these the guerdons of the greatest minds,
To make them hope and yet betray their hap,
To make them clime to ouerthrow them straight?
Accurst thy wreake, thy wrath, thy bale, thy wheele,
That makst me sigh the sorrowes that I feele.
Untroden paths my feete shall rather trace,
Than wrest my succours from inconstant hands.
Rebounding Rocks shall rather ring my ruth,
Than these Campanian piles where terrors bide.
And nature that hath lift my throne so hie,
Shall witnes Marius triumphs if he die.
But shee that gaue the Lictors rod and axe,
To wait my sixe times Consulship in Rome,
will not pursue where erst she flattered so,
Minturnum then farewell for I must goe,
But thinke for to repent you of your no.

PAUSANIUS

Nay stay my Lord and daine in priuate here,
To waight a message of more better worth,
Your age and trauels must haue some releefe,
And be not wroth, for greater men than we
Haue feared Rome and Romaine tirranie.

MARIUS
You talke it now like men confirmde in faith,
well let me trie the fruits of your discourse,
For care my minde and paine my bodie wrongs.

PAUSANIUS
Then Fauorinus shut his Lordship up,
within some secret chamber in the state,
Meane while we will consult to keepe him safe,
And worke some secret meanes for his supplie.

MARIUS
Be trustie Lords, if not I can but die.

[Exit **MARIUS**

PAUSANIUS
Poore haples Romaine, little wottest thou,
The wearie end of thine oppressed life.

LUCIUS
Why my Pausanius, what imports these words?

PAUSANIUS
Oh Lucius age hath printed in my thoughts,
A memorie of many troubles past,
The greatest townes and Lords of Asia,
Haue stood on tickle tearmes through simple truth,
The Rhodian records weil can witnes this.
Then to preuent our meanes of ouerthrow,
Finde out some stranger that may sodainely,
Enter the chamber where as Marius lies,
And cut him short, the present of whose head
Shall make the Romaines praise vs for our truth,
And Scilla prest to graunt vs priuiledge.

LUCIUS
A barbarous act to wrong the men that trust,

PAUSANIUS
In Countries cause in iustice proueth iust.
Come Lucius let not sillie thought of right,

Subiect our Citie to the Romaines might:
For why you know in Marius onely end,
Rome will reward and Scilla will be friend.

LUCIUS
Yet all successions will vs discommend.

[Exeunt.

[Enter **MARIUS** the younger: **CETHEGUS**: **LECTORIUS** with other Romaine **LORDS** and **SOULDIERS**.

MARIUS jnr
The way ward Ladie of this wicked world.
That leads in luckles triumph wretched men,
My Romaine friends hath forced our desires,
And framde our minds to brooke too base reliefe,
What land or Libian desert is vnsought,
To finde my father Marius and your friend:
Yea they whom true relent could neuer touch,
These fierce Numidians hearing our mishaps,
Weepe flouds of mone to waile our wretched fates.
Thus we that erst with terrors did attaint,
The Bactrian bounds and in our Romaine warres,
Enforst the barbarous borderers of the Alpes,
To tremble with the terrors of our lookes.
Now flie poore men affrighted with our harmes,
Seeking amidst the desert rocks and dens,
For him that whilom in our Capitoll,
Euen with a becke commaunded Asia.
Thou wofull sonne of such a famous man,
Vnsheath thy sword, conduct these warlike men
To Rome, vnhappie Mistris of our harmes:
And there since tyrants powre hath thee opprest,
And robd thee of thy father, friends and all,
So die vndaunted, killing of thy foes,
That were the offspring of these wretched woes.

LECTORIUS
Why how now Marius, will you mate vs thus;
That with content aduenture for your loue?
Why Noble youth resolue your selfe on this,
That sonne and father both haue friends in Rome:
That seeke olde Marius rest and your reliefe.

MARIUS jnr
Lectorius, friends are geason now adaies,
And grow to fume before they tast the fire:
Aduersities bereaving mans availes,

They flie like feathers dallying in the winde,
They rise like bubbles in a stormie raine,
Swelling in words and flying faith and deedes.

CETHEGUS
How fortunate art thou my louely Lord,
That in thy youth maist reape the fruits of age,
And hauing lost occasions hold-fast now,
Maist learne hereafter how to entertaine her well:
But sodaine hopes doo swarme about my hart,
Be merry Romaines see where from the Coast,
A wearie messenger doth poast him fast.

[Enter Cynnas' **SLAVE** with a letter inclosed posting in hast.

LECTORIUS
It should be Cynnas slave or else I erre,
For in his forhead I behold the scar,
Wherewith he marketh still his barbarous swaines.

MARIUS jnr
Oh stay him good Lectorius for me seeme,
His great post hast some pleasure should present.

LECTORIUS
Sirra art thou of Rome?

SLAVE
Perhaps Sir no?

LECTORIUS
Without perhaps say Sirra is it so?

SLAVE
This is Lectorius Marius friend I trow,
Yet were I best to learne the certainetie,
Lest some dissembling foes should me disery.

MARIUS jnr
Sirra leaue off this foolish dalliance,
Lest with my sword I wake you from your trance.

SLAVE
Oh happie man, Oh labours well atchieude,
How hath this chance my wearie lims reuiude:
Oh Noble Marius, Oh Princelie Marius.

MARIUS jnr

What meanes this Pesant by his great reioice.

SLAVE
Oh worthy Romaine, many months haue past,
Since Cynna now the Consul and my Lord,
Hath sent me forth to seeke thy friends and thee:
All Libia with our Romaine Presidents,
Numidia full of unfrequented waies,
These wearie limbs haue troad to seeke you out,
And now occasion pitying of my paines,
I late arriude upon this wished shore,
Found out a Sailer borne in Capua,
That told me how your Lordship past this way,

MARIUS jnr
A happie labor worthie some reward,
How fares thy master? whats the newes at Rome?

SLAVE
Pull out the pike from off this jauelin top,
And there are tidings for these Lords and thee,

MARIUS jnr
A pollicie beseeming Cynna well:
Lectorius read, and breake these letters up.

Letters.
To his honourable frend Marius the yonger greeting.
Being Consull (for the welfare both of father and sonne, wish other thy accomplices) I haue under an honest policie since my instalment in the Consulship, caused all Scillas frends that were indifferent with the other neighbring Cities to reuolt: Octavius my fellow Consul with the rest of the Senate mistrusting me, and hearing how I sought to unite the old Citizens with the new, hath wrought much trouble, but to no effect. I hope the souldiers of Capua shall follow our faction, for Scilla hearing of these hurly-burlies is hasting homeward verie fortunate in his warres against Mithridates. And it is to be feared, that some of his frends here haue certified him of my proceedings, and purpose to restore you. Cethegus and Lectorius I heare say are with you. Censorinus and Albinovanus will shortly visit you. Therefore hast and seeke out your father, who is now as I heare about Minturnum. Leuie what power you can with all expedition, and stay not.
Rome the Kalends of December.
Your unfained frend,
Cynna Consull.

MARIUS jnr
Yea Fortune, shall yong Marius clime aloft,
Then woe to my repining foes in Rome,
And if I liue (sweete Queene of change) thy shrines,
Shall shine with beautie midst the Capitoll,
Lectorius, tell me what were best be done.

LECTOR
To sea my Lord, seeke your warlike Sire,
Send backe this pesant with your full pretence,
And thinke alreadie that our paines haue end,
Since Cynna with his followers is your frend.

MARIUS jnr
Yea Romanes we will furrow through the fome
Of swelling flouds, and to the sacred Twins
Make sacrifice to shield our ships from stormes.
Follow me Lords, come gentle messenger,
Thou shalt haue gold and glorie for thy paines.

[Exeunt.

ACTUS TERTIUS

SCENA PRIMA

Enter **CYNNA, OCTAVIUS, MARK ANTHONY, LICTORS, CITIZENS.**

CYNNA
Upbraiding Senators bewitcht with wit,
That terme true iustice innouation:
You ministers of Scillas mad conceipts,
Will Consulls thinke you stoope to your controules?
These yonger Citizens, my fellow Lords,
Bound to maintaine both Marius and his sonne.
Craue but their due, and will be held as good
For priuiledge, as those of elder age:
For they are men conformd to feats of armes,
That haue both wit and courage to commaund.
These fauorites of Octavius, what with age
And palsies shake their iauelins in their hands,
Like hartlesse men attainted all with feare:
And should they then ouer-top the youth.
No, nor this Consull, nor Marke Anthonie,
Shall make my followers faint, or loose their right,
But I will haue them equall with the best.

MARK ANTHONY
Why then the Senates name (whose reuerence
Hath blazd our vertues midst the Westerne Ile)
Must be obseurde by Cynnas forced powre.
O Citizens, are lawes of Countrey left?

Is iustice banisht from this Capitoll?
Must we poore fathers see your trooping bands
Enter the sacred Synode of this state.
Oh brutish fond presumptions of this age,
Rome would the mischiefes might obscure my life,
So I might counsaile Consulls to be wise.
Why Countri-men wherein consists this strife?
Forsooth the yonger Citizens will rule,
The old mens heads are dull and addle now:
And in elections youth will beare the sway?
O Cynna, see I not the wofull fruits
Of these ambitious stratagems begun,
Each flattring tongue that dallieth pretie words,
Shall change our fortunes and our states at once.
Had I ten thousand tongues to talke the care,
So manie eyes to weepe their wofull misse,
So manie pennes to write these manie wrongs:
My tongue your thoughts, my eyes your teares shuld moue,
My pen your paines by reasons should approue.

CYNNA
Why Anthonie, seale up those sugred lips,
For I will bring my purpose to effect.

MARK ANTHONY
Doth Cynna like to interrupt me then?

CYNNA
I Cynna sir, will interrupt you now,
I tell thee Marke, old Marius is at hand,
The verie patron of this happie law,
Who will reuenge thy cunning eloquence.

MARK ANTHONY
I talke not I to please or him or thee,
But what I speake, I thinke and practice too:
Twere better Scilla learnt to mend in Rome,
Than Marius come to tyrannize in Rome.

OCTAVIUS
Nay Marius shall not tyrannize in Rome,
Old Citizens, as Scilla late ordaind,
King Tullius lawes shall take their full effect,
The best and aged men shall in their choice,
Both beare the day and firme election.

CYNNA
Oh braue Octavius you will beard me then,

The elder Consull and old Marius frend,
And these Italian freemen must be wrongd.
First shall the frute of all thine honors faile,
And this my ponyard shall dispatch thy life.

LEPIDUS
Such insolence was neuer seene in Rome:
Nought wanteth here but name to make a King.

OCTAVIUS
Strike villaine if thou list, for I am prest,
To make as deepe a surrow in thy brest.

YOUNG CITIZEN
The yong mens voices shal preuaile my lords.

OLD CITIZEN
And we will firme our honors by our blouds.

[Thunder.

MARK ANTHONY
O false ambitious pride in yong and old:
Harke how the heauens our follies hath contrould.

OLD CITIZEN
What shall we yeeld for this religious feare?

MARK ANTHONY
If not religious feare, what may represse
These wicked passions, wretched Citizens.
O Rome, poore Rome, unmeet for these misdeedes,
I see contempt of heauens will breed a crosse:
Sweete Cynna gouerne rage with reuerence.

[Thunder.

O fellow Citizens, be more aduisde.

LEPIDUS
We charge you Consulls now dissolve the Court
The Gods contemne this brawle and civil warres.

OCTAVIUS
We will submit our honors to their wills:
You ancient Citizens come follow mee.

[Exit **OCTAVIUS**, with him **MARK ANTHONY** & **LEPIDUS**.

CYNNA

High Ioue himselfe hath done too much for thee,
Els should this blade abate thy royaltie.
Well yong Italian Citizens take hart,
He is at hand that will maintaine your right:
That entring in these fatall gates of Rome,
Shall make them tremble that disturbe you now.
You of Preneste and of Formiae,
With other neighbring Cities in Campania,
Prepare to entertaine and succor Marius.

CITIZEN

For him we liue, for him we meane to die.

[Exeunt.

[Enter old **MARIUS** with his **JAILOR** keeper, & two **SOULDIERS**.

MARIUS pater

Haue these Minturnians then so cruelly,
Presumd so great iniustice gainst their frends?

JAILOR

I Marius, all our Nobles haue decreed
To send thy head a present unto Rome.

MARIUS pater

A Tantals present it will proue my frend,
Which with a little smarting stresse will end
Old Marius life, when Rome it selfe at last,
Shall rue my losse, and then reuenge my death.
But tell me Iailer, couldst thou be content,
In being Marius for to brooke this wrong.

JAILOR

The high estate your Lordship once did wield,
The manie frends that fawnd when fortune smild,
Your great promotions, and your mightie welth:
These (were I Marius) would amate me so,
As losse of them would vexe me more than death.

MARIUS pater

Is Lordship then so great a blisse my frend?

JAILOR

No title may compare with princely rule.

MARIUS pater
Are frends so faithfull pledges of delight?

JAILOR
What better comforts than are faithfull frends?

MARIUS pater
Is welth a meane to lengthen liues content?

JAILOR
Where great possessions bide, what care can tutch?

MARIUS pater
These stales of fortune are the common plagues
That still mislead the thoughts of simple men.
The shepheard swaine that midst his country cote,
Deludes his broken slumbers by his toyle,
Thinkes Lordship sweete, where care with lordship dwelt
The trustfull man that builds on trothles vowes,
Whose simple thoughts are crost with scornfull nayes,
Together weepes the losse of welth and frend:
So Lordship, frends, welth, spring and perish fast,
Where death alone yeelds happie life at last.
O gentle gouernor of my contents,
Thou sacred chieftaine of our Capitoll,
Who in thy christall orbes with glorious gleameS,
Lendst lookes of pitie mixt with maiestie,
See wofull Marius carefull for his sonne,
Carelesse of lordship, welth or worldly meanes,
Content to liue, yet liuing still to die:
Whose nerues and veynes, whose sinewes by the sword
Must loose their workings through distempering stroake:
But yet whose minde in spight of fate and all,
Shall liue by fame although the bodie fall.

JAILOR
Why mourneth Marius this recurelesse chance?

MARIUS pater
I pre thee Iailer wouldst thou gladly die?

JAILOR
If needes, I would.

MARIUS pater
Yet were you loath to trie.

JAILOR

Why noble Lord, when goods, frends, fortune faile
What more than death might wofull man auaile?

MARIUS pater
Who calls for death (my frend) for all his scornes,
With Aesops slaue will leaue his bush of thornes.
But since these traitrous Lords will haue my head,
Their Lordships here upon this homely bed,
Shall finde me sleeping, breathing forth my breath;
Till they their shame, and I my fame attaine by death.
Liue gentle Marius to reuenge my wrong,
And sirrha see they stay not ouer-long.
For he that earst hath conquered kingdomes many,
Disdaines in death to be subdude by anie.

[He lies downe.

[Enter **LUCIUS FAVORINUS, PAUSANIUS**, with **PEDRO**, a French-man.

JAILOR
The most undanted words that euer were.
The mightie thoughts of his imperious minde,
Do wound my hart with terror and remorse.

PAUSANIUS
Tis desperate, not perfect noblenes,
For to a man that is preparde to die,
The heart should rent, the sleepe should leaue the eye:
But say Pedro, will you doo the deed?

PEDRO
Mon monsieurs perla sang dieu, mee will make a trou so large in ce belly, dat he sal cry hough come une porceau. Featre delay, il a true me fadre, hee kill my modre. Faith a my trote mon espee: fera le fay dun sol dat, Sau, sau, Ieieuera, come il founta pary, me will make a spitch-cocke of his persona.

FAVORINUS
If he haue slaine thy father and thy frends,
The greater honor shall betide the deed:
For to reuenge on righteous estimate,
Beseemes the honor of a French mans name.

PEDRO
Mes messiers, de fault auoir argent, me no point de argent, no point kill Marius.

PAUSANIUS
Thou shalt haue forty crowns, wil that content thee?

PEDRO

Quarante escus, per le pied de Madam, me giue more dan foure to se prettie damosele, dat haue le dulces tettinos, leleures cymbrines. Oh they be fines.

FAVORINUS
Great is the hire and little is the paine,
Make therefore quicke dispatch, and looke for gaine.
See where he lies in drawing on his death,
Whose cries by gentle slumber sealed up,
Present no dreadfull visions to his hart.

PEDRO
Bien monsieur, le demourera content. Maries tu es mort. Speake dy preres in dy sleepe, for me sall cut off your head from your espaules before you wake. Qui es stia, what kinde a man be dis.

FAVORINUS
Why what delaies are these, why gaze ye thus?

PEDRO
Nostre dame, Iesu estiene, oh my siniors der be a great diable in ce eies, qui dart de flame, and with de voice d'un beare, cries out, Villaine dare you kill Marius. Ie tremble: aida me siniors, autrement I shall be murdred.

PAUSANIUS
What sodaine madnes daunts this stranger thus?

PEDRO
Oh me no can kill Marius, me no dare kill Marius: adieu messiers, me be dead si ie touche Marius, Marius est une diable. Iesu Maria saua moy.

[Exit **FUGIENS.**

PAUSANIUS
What furie haunts this wretch on sodaine thus?

FAVORINUS
Ah my Pausanius I haue often heard,
That yonder Marius in his infancie
Was borne to greater fortunes than we deeme:
For being scarce from out his cradle crept,
And sporting pretely with his compeeres,
On sodaine seuen yong Eagles soard amaine,
And kindly pearcht upon his tender lap.
His parents wondring at this strange euent,
Tooke counsaile of the Southsaiers in this,
Who told them that these seuen-fold Eagles flight,
Fore figured his seuen times Consulship:
And we our selues (except bewitcht with pride)
Haue seene him sixe times in the Capitoll

Accompanyd with rods and axes too.
And some diuine instinct so presseth mee,
That sore I tremble till I set him free.

PAUSANIUS
The like assaults attaint my wandring minde.
Seeing our bootlesse warre with matchlesse fate,
Let vs intreat him to forsake our towne,
So shall we gaine a frend of Rome and him:

[**MARIUS pater** awaketh.

But marke how happely he doth awake.

MARIUS pater
What, breath I yet pore man, with mounting sight
Choaking the riuers of my restlesse eies?
Or is their rage restraind with matchlesse ruth?
See how amazd these angrie Lords behold
The poore confused lookes of wretched Marius.
Minturnians why delaies your headsman thus
To finish up this ruthfull tragedie?

FAVORINUS
Far be it Marius from our thoughts or hands
To wrong the man protected by the Gods:
Liue happie (Marius) so thou leaue our towne.

MARIUS pater
And must I wrestle once againe with fate?
Or will these Princes dally with mine age?

PAUSANIUS
No matchles Romane, thine approued minde
That earst hath altred our ambitious wrong
Must flourish still, and we thy seruants liue
To see thy glories like the swelling tides
Exceed the bounds of Fate and Romane rule.
Yet leaue vs Lord, and seeke some safer shed,
Where more secure thou maist preuent mishaps:
For great pursuits and troubles thee awaite.

MARIUS pater
Ye piteous powres that with succesfull hopes,
And gentle counsailes thwart my deepe dispaires:
Olde Marius to your mercies recommends
His hap, his life, his hazard and his sonne.
Minturnians, I will hence, and you shall flie

Occasions of those troubles you expect.
Dreame not on dangers that haue faud my life:
Lordings adieu, from walls to woods I wend,
To hills, dales, rockes, my wrong for to commend.

[Exit.

FAVORINUS
Fortune vouchsafe thy manie cares to end.

[Exeunt.

PRIMA SCENA

Enter **SCILLA** in triumph in his chare triumphant of gold, drawen by foure **MOORES**, before the chariot: his colours, his crest, his captaines, his prisoners: **ARCATHIUS MITHRIDATES** son, **ARISTION**, **ARCHELAUS**, bearing crownes of gold, and manacled. After the chariot, his **SOULDIERS** bands, **BASILLUS**, **LUCRETIUS, LUCULLUS**: besides prisoners of diuers Nations, and sundry disguises.

SCILLA
You men of Rome, my fellow mates in Armes,
Whose three yeares prowesse, pollicie, and warre,
One hundreth three score thousand men at Armes
Hath ouerthrowne and murthered in the field:
Whose valours to the Empire hath restorde,
All Grecia, Asia, and Ionia.
With Macedonia subiect to our foe:
You see the froward customes of our state,
Who measuring not our many toiles abroad,
Sit in their Cells imagining our harmes,
Replenishing our Romaine friends with feare.
Yea, Scilla worthy friends, whose fortunes, toiles,
And stratagems these strangers may report,
Is by false Cynna and his factious friends.
Reuilde, condemnde, and crost without a cause.
Yet (Romaines) Marius must returne to Rome,
Of purpose to upbraid your Generall.
But this undaunted minde that neuer droopt:
This forward bodie formd to suffer toile,
Shall hast to Rome where euerie foe shall rue,
The rash disgrace both of my selfe and you:

LUCRETIUS
And may it be that those seditious braines,
Imagine these presumptuous purposes?

SCILLA

And may it be? why man and wilt thou doubt,
Where Scilla daines these dangers to auerre?
Sirrha except not so, misdoubt not so,
See here Ancharius letters reade the lines,
And say Lucretius that I fauour thee,
That darest but suspect thy Generall,
Read the letters and deliuer them.

LUCRETIUS

The case conceald hath moued the more misdoubt,
Yet pardon my presumptions worthy Scilla,
That to my griefe haue read these hideous harmes,

SCILLA

Tut my Lucretius, fortunes ball is tost,
To forme the storie of my fatall powre:
Rome shall repent, babe, mother, shall repent,
Aire weeping clowdie sorrowes shall repent,
wind breathing many sighings shall repent
To see those stormes concealed in my brest,
Reflect the hideous flames of their unrest:
But words are vaine, and cannot quell our wrongs,
Briefe periods serue for them that needs must postit.
Lucullus since occasion calls me hence,
And all our Romaine senate thinke it meete,
That thou pursue the warres I haue begun,
As by their letters I am certified,
I leaue thee Fimbrias Legions to conduct,
with this prouiso, that in ruling still,
You thinke on Scilla and his curtesies.

LUCULLUS

The waightie charge of this continued warre,
Though strange it seeme, and ouer great to wield,
I will accept it so the Armie please.

SOULDIERS

Happie & fortunate be Lucullus our Generall.

SCILLA

If he be Scillas friend, els not at all:
For otherwise the man were ill bested,
That gaining glories straight should lose his head.
But souldiers since I needly must to Rome,
Basillus vertues shall haue recompence.
Lo here the wreath Valerius for thy paines,

Who first didst enter Archilous trench:
This pledge of vertue sirrha shall approue,
Thy vertues, and confirme me in thy loue.

BASILLUS
Happie be Scilla, if no foe to Rome.

SCILLA
I like no iffs from such a simple groome,
I will be happie in despite of state,
And why? because I neuer feared fate.
But come Arcathius for your fathers sake,
Enioyne your fellow Princes to their taskes,
And helpe to succour these my wearie bones.
Tut blush not man, a greater state than thou,
Shall pleasure Scilla in more baser sort.
Aristion is a iolly timberd man,
Fit to conduct the chariot of a King.
Why be not squeamish, for it shall goe hard,
But I will giue you all a great reward.

ARCATHIUS
Humbled by fate like wretched men we yeeld

SCILLA
Arcathius these are fortunes of the field.
Beleeue me these braue Captyues draw by art,
And I will thinke upon their good desart.
But stay you strangers, and respect my words,
Fond hartles men, what folly haue I seene:
For feare of death can Princes entertaine
Such bastard thoughts, that now from glorious armes
Vouchsafe to draw like oxen in a plough.
Arcathius I am sure Mithridates
Will hardly brooke the scandall of his name:
Twere better in Picaeo to haue died
Aristion, than amidst our legions thus to draw.

ARISTION
I tell thee Scilla, captiues haue no choice,
And death is dreadfull to a caytiue man.

SCILLA
In such imperfect mettals as is yours.
But Romanes that are still allurde by fame,
Chuse rather death than blemish of their name,
But I haue hast, and therefore will reward you.
Goe souldiers, with as quicke dispatch as may be,

Hasten their death, and bring them to their end,
And say in this that Scilla is your frend.

ARCATHIUS
Oh ransome thou our lives sweet conqueror.

SCILLA
Fie foolish men, why flie you happines,
Desire you still to lead a seruile life.
Dare you not buy delights with little paines.
Well, for thy fathers sake Arcathius,
I will preferre thy triumphs with the rest.
Goe take them hence, and when we meete in hell,
Then tell me Princes if I did not well.

[Exeunt **MILITES**.

Lucullus, thus these mightie foes are downe,
Now striue thou for the king of Pontus crowne.
I will to Rome, goe thou, and with thy traine,
Pursue Mithridates till he be slaine.

LUCULLUS
With fortunes help, go calme thy countries woes
Whilst I with these seeke out our mightie foes.

[Enter **MARIUS** solus from the Numidian mountaines, feeding on rootes.

MARIUS pater
Thou that hast walkt with troops of flocking frends,
Now wandrest midst the laborynth of woes,
Thy best repast with manie sighing ends,
And none but fortune all these mischiefes knowes.
Like to these stretching mountaines clad with snow,
No sun-shine of content my thoughts approcheth:
High spyre their tops, my hopes no height do know,
But mount so high as time their tract reprocheth:
They finde their spring, where winter wrongs my minde:
They weepe their brookes, I wast my cheekes with teares.
Oh foolish fate, too froward and unkinde,
Mountaines haue peace, where mournfull be my yeres:
Yet high as they my thoughts some hopes would borrow,
But when I count the euening end with sorrow.
Death in Minturnum threatned Marius head,
Hunger in these Numidian mountaines dwells:
Thus with preuention hauing mischiefe fled,
Old Marius findes a world of manie hells.
Such as poore simple wits haue oft repinde,

But I will quell by vertues of the minde.
Long yeres misspent in manie luckles chances,
Thoughts full of wroth, yet little worth succeeding,
These are the meanes for those whom fate aduances:
But I, whose wounds are fresh, my hart still bleeding,
Liues to intreate this blessed boone from fate,
That I might die with griefe to liue in state.
Sixe hundreth sonnes with solitarie walkes,
I still haue sought for to delude my paine,
And frendly Eccho answering to my talkes,
Rebounds the accent of my ruth againe:
She (curteous Nymph) the wofull Romane pleaseth,
Els no consorts but beasts my paines appeaseth.
Each day she answeres, in yond neighbring mountaine,
I doo expect reporting of my sorrow,
Whilst lifting up her lockes from out the fountaine,
She answereth to my questions euen and morrow:
Whose sweete rebounds my sorrowes to remoue,
To please my thoughts I meane for to approue.
Sweet Nymph draw nere thou kind & gentle Eccho. Eccho.
What help to ease my wearie paines haue I? I.
What comfort in distres to calme my griefes? griefes.
Sweet Nymph these griefes are growne before I thought so? I thought so.
Thus Marius liues disdaind of all the Gods. Oads.
With deepe dispaire late ouertaken wholy. Oly.
And wil the heavens be neuer wel appeased? appeased.
What meane haue they left me to cure my smart? art.
Nought better fits old Marius mind then war, then war.
Then full of hope say Eccho, shall I goe? goe.
Is anie better fortune then at hand, at hand.
Then farewell Eccho, gentle Nymph farewel. farewell.
Oh pleasing folly to a pensiue man.
Well I will rest fast by this shadie tree.
Waiting the end that fate allotteth mee. sit downe.

[Enter **MARIUS** the sonne, **ALBINOVANUS**, **CETHEGUS**, **LECTORIUS**, with **SOULDIERS**.

MARIUS jnr
My countrimen and fauorites of Rome,
This melancholy desart where we meete,
Resembleth well yong Marius restles thoughts.
Here dreadfull silence, solitarie caues,
No chirping birds with solace singing sweetlie,
Are harbored for delight: but from the oake
Leaueles and saples through decaying age,
The scotch-owle chants her fatall boding layes.
Within my brest, care, danger, sorrow dwells,
Hope and reuenge sit hammering in my hart,

The balefull babes of angrie Nemesis
Dispearse their furious fires upon my soule.

LECTORIUS
Fie Marius, are you discontented still,
When as occasion fauoreth your desire?
Are not these noble Romanes come from Rome?
Hath not the state recald your father home?

MARIUS jnr
And what of this, what profit may I reape,
That want my father to conduct vs home.

LECTORIUS
My Lord, take hart, no doubt this stormie slawe
That Neptune sent to cast vs on this shore.
Shall end these discontentments at the last.

MARIUS pater
Whom see mine eyes, what is not yon my son?

MARIUS jnr
what solitarie father walketh there?

MARIUS pater
It is my sonne, these are my frends I see:
what haue forepining cares, so changed mee?
Or are my lookes; distempred through the paines
And agonies that issue from my hart?
Fie Marius, frolicke man, thou must to Rome,
There to reuenge thy wrongs and waight thy tombe.

MARIUS jnr
Now fortune frowne, & palter if thou please,
Romanes behold my father and your frend.
Oh father.

MARIUS pater
Marius thou art fitly met:
Albinouanus and my other frends,
What newes at Rome? what fortune brought you hither?

ALBINOVANUS
My Lord, the Consull Cynna hath restord
The doubtfull course of your betrayed state,
And waits you prresent swift approch to Rome,
Your foe man Scilla poasteth verie fast,
With good successe from Pontus to preuent

Your speedie entrance into Italy.
The neighbring Cities are your verie frends,
Nought rests my Lord, but you depart from hence.

MARIUS jnr
How manie desart waies hath Marius sought,
How manie Cities haue I visited,
To finde my father, and releeue his wants?

MARIUS pater
My sonne, I quite thy trauells with my loue,
And Lords and Citizens we will to Rome,
And ioyne with Cynna haue your shipping here?
What are these souldiers bent to die with mee?

SOULDIER
Content to pledge our liues for Marius.

LECTORIUS
My Lord, here in the next adioyning port,
Our ships are rigd and readie for to saile.

MARIUS pater
Then let vs saile unto Hetruria,
And cause our frends the Germanes to reuolt,
And get some Tuscans to increase our power.
Deserts farewell come Romanes let vs goe,
A scourge for Rome that hath deprest vs so,

[Exeunt.

SCENA SECONDA

Enter **MARK ANTHONY, LEPIDUS, OCTAVIUS, FLACCUS, SENATORS.**

OCTAVIUS
What helpes my Lords to ouerhale these cares?
What meanes or motions may these mischiefe end?
You see how Cynna that should succor Rome,
Hath leuied armes to bring a traitor in.
O worthlesse traitor, woe to thine and thee,
That thus disquieteth both Rome and vs.

MARK ANTHONY
Octavius these are scourges for our sinnes,
These are but ministers to heape our plagues:

These mutinies are gentle meanes and waies,
Whereby the heavens our heauie errors charmes,
Then with content and humbled eyes, behold
The christall shining globe of glorious loue:
And since we perish through our owne misdeedes,
Go let vs flourish in our frutefull praiers.

LEPIDUS
Midst these confusions mighty men of Rome,
Why wast we out these troubles all in words,
Weepe not your harmes, but wend we straight so armes,
Loe Distia spoyld, see Marius at our gate:
And shall we die like milksops dreaming thus?

OCTAVIUS
A bootles warre to see our countrey spoild.

LEPIDUS
Fruteles is dalliance whereas dangers bee.

MARK ANTHONY
My Lord, may courage wait on conquered men?

LEPIDUS
I euen in death most courage doth appeare.

OCTAVIUS
Then wanting death I meane to seate me here,
Hoping that Consulls name and feare of lawes,
Shall iustifie my conscience and my cause,

[Enter **MESSENGER**.

Now sirrha, what confused lookes are these,
What tidings bringest thou of dreriment?

MESSENGER
My Lords, the Consull Cynna with his friends
Haue let in Marius by Via Appia,
Whose souldiers wast and murther all they meete,
Who with the Consull and his other frends
With expedition hasteth to this place.

MARK ANTHONY
Then to the downfall of my happines,
Then to the ruine of this Citie Rome.
But if mine inward ruth were laid in sight,
My streames of teares should drowne my foes despight.

OCTAVIUS

Courage Lord Anthony, if Fortune please,
She will and can these troubles soone appease.
But if her backward frownes approch vs nie,
Resolue with vs with honor for to die.

LEPIDUS

No storme of fate shall bring my sorrowes downe,
But if that Fortune list, why let her frowne.

MARK ANTHONY

Where state's opprest by cruell tyrants bee,
Old Anthony, there is no place for thee.

[Drum strike within:

Harke, by this thundring noyse of threatning drums,
Marius with all his faction hether comes.

[Enter **MARIUS**, his Sonne, **CYNNA**, **CETHEGUS**, **LECTORIOUS** with **SOULDIERS**: upon sight of whom **MARK ANTHONY** presently flies.

OCTAVIUS

Then like a traitor he shall know ere long,
In leuying armes he doth his countrey wrong.

MARIUS pater

And haue we got the goale of honor now,
And in despight of Consulls entred Rome?
Then rouze thee Marius, leaue thy ruthfull thoughts:
And for thy manie toiles and cares sustaind,
Afflict thy foes with twice as many paines.
Goe souldiers seeke out Bebius and his frends,
Attilius, Munitorius with the rest,
Cut off their heads, for they did crosse me once:
And if your care can compasse my decree,
Remember that same fugitiue Marke Anthony,
Whose fatall end shall be my frutefull peace.
I tell thee Cynna, nature armeth beasts
With iust reuenge, and lendeth in their kindes
Sufficient warlike weapons of defence:
If then by nature beasts reuenge their wrong,
Both heauens and nature grant me vengeance now,
Yet whilst I liue and sucke this subtill aire
That lendeth breathing coolenes to my lights,
The register of all thy righteous acts,
Thy paines, thy toiles, thy trauells for my sake,

Shall dwell by kinde impressions in my hart,
And I with linkes of true unfained lone
Will locke these Romane fauorites in my brest,
And liue to hazard life for their releefe.

CYNNA
My Lord, your safe and swift returne to Rome,
Makes Cynna fortunate and well appaid,
Who through the false suggestions of my foes,
Was made a coffer of a Consull here:
Lo where he sits commanding in his throue,
That wronged Marius, me, and all these Lords.

MARIUS jnr
To quite his loue, Cynna let me alone,
How fare these Lords that lumping pouting proud
Imagine how to quell me with their lookes.
No welcome sirs, is Marius thought so base?
Why stand you looking babies in my face?
Who welcomes mee, him Marius makes his frend:
Who lowres on mee, him Marius meanes to end.

FLACCUS
Happie and fortunate thy returne to Rome.

LEPIDUS
And long Marius liue with fame in Rome.

MARIUS pater
I thanke you curteous Lords that are so kinde.

MARIUS jnr
But why endures your Grace that brauing mate
To sit and face vs in his roabes of state.

MARIUS pater
My sonne he is a Consull at the least,
And grauitie becomes Octavius best.
But Cynna would in yonder emptie seat,
You would for Marius freedome once intreate.
Cynna presseth up, and Octavius staieth him.

OCTAVIUS
Auant thou traitor, proud and insolent,
How darest thou presse nere ciuill gouernment.

MARIUS pater
Why Master Consull, are you growne so hot?

He haue a present cooling card for you.
Be therefore well aduisde, and moue me not:
For though by you I was exilde from Rome,
And in the desart from a Princes seate
Left to bewaile ingratitudes of Rome.
Though I haue knowne your thirshe throates haue longd
To baine their selues in my distilling blood.
Yet Marius Sirs, hath pitie ioynd with powre:
Loe here the Imperiall Ensigne which I wield,
That waueth mercie to my wishers well:
And more see here the dangerous trote of warre,
That at the point is steeld with ghastly death.

OCTAVIUS
Thou exile, threatnest thou a Consull then?
Lictors, goe draw him hence: such brauing mates,
Are not to boast their armes in quiet states.

MARIUS pater
Go draw me hence. What no relent Octavius?

MARIUS jnr
My Lord what hart in durate with reuenge,
Could leaue this lossell, threatning murther thus?
Vouchsafe me leaue to taint that traitors seate
With flowing streames of his contagious blood.

OCTAVIUS
The fathers sonne, I know him by his talke,
That scolds in words when fingers cannot walke.
But Ioue I hope will one day send to Rome
The blessed Patron of this Monarchie,
Who will reuenge iniustice by his sword.

CYNNA
Such brauing hopes, such cursed arguments,
So strict command, such arrogant controwles.
Suffer me Marius, that am Consull now,
To doo thee iustice, and confound the wretch.

MARIUS pater
Cynna, you know I am a priuate man,
That still submit my censures to your will.

CYNNA
Then souldiers draw this traitor from the throne,
And let him die, for Cynna wills it so.

MARIUS jnr
I now my Cynna, noble Consull speakes,
Octavius, your checkes shall cost you deare.

OCTAVIUS
And let me die for Cynna wills it so?
Is then the reuerence of this robe contemnnd?
Are these associates of so small regard?
Why then Octavius willingly consents,
To entertaine the sentence of his death.
But let the proudest traitor worke his will,
I feare no strokes, but here will sit me still.
Since iustice sleepes, since tyrants raigne in Rome,
Octavius longs for death to die for Rome.

CYNNA
Then strike him where he sits, then hale him hence.
A souldier stabs him, he is caried away.

OCTAVIUS
Heauens punish Cynnas pride and thy offence.

CYNNA
Now is he falne that threatned Marius,
Now will I sit and plead for Marius.

MARIUS pater
Thou doost me iustice Cynna, for you see
These peeres of Rome haue late exiled mee.

LEPIDUS
Your Lordship doth iniustice to accuse
Those who in your behalfe did not offend.

FLACCUS
We grieue to see the aged Marius
Stand like a priuate man in view of Rome.

CYNNA
Then bid him sit, and loe an emptie place,
Reuoke his exile, firme his gouernment,
And so preuent your farther detriment,

LEPIDUS
We will accompt both Marius and his frends,
His sonne and all his followers free in Rome:
And since we see the dangerous times at hand,
And here of Scillas confidence and hast,

And know his hate and rancor to these Lords,
And him create for Consull to preuent
The policies of Scilla and his frends.

CYNNA
Then both confirmd by state and full consent,
The rods and axe to Marius I present,
And here inuest thee with the Consulls pall.

FLACCUS
Long, fortunate and happie life betide
Old Marius in his seuenfold Consulship.

MARIUS jnr
And so let Marius liue and gouerne Rome,
As cursed Scilla neuer looke on Rome.

MARIUS pater
Then placde in Consuls throne, you Romane states

[He takes his seate.

Recald from banishment by your decrees,
Enstald in this imperiall seate to rule,
Old Marius thankes his frends and fauorites:
From whom this finall fauor he requires,
That seeing Scilla by his murthrous blade
Brought fierce seditions first to head in Rome,
And forced lawes to banish innocents:
I craue by course of reason and desert,
That he may be proclaimd as earst was I,
A traitor and an enemie of Rome:
Let all his frends be banisht out of towne:
Then cutting off the branch where troubles spring,
Rome shall haue peace and plentie in her walls.

CYNNA
In equitie it needes must be my frends,
That one be guiltie of our common harmes:
And since that Marius is accounted free,
Scilla with all his frends must traitors bee.

MARIUS jnr
My fathers reasons Romanes are of force:
For if you see and liue not too secure,
You know that in so great a state as this,
Two mightie foes can neuer well agree.

LEPIDUS
Then let us seeke to please our Consull first,
And then prepare to keep the exile out.
Cynna, as Marius and these Lords agree,
Firme this Edict, and let it passe for mee.

CYNNA
Then Romanes, in the name of all this state,
I here proclaime and publish this decree:
That Scilla with his frends, allies and all•
Are banisht exiles, traitors unto Rome.
And to extinguish both his name and state,
We will his house be raced to the ground,
His goods confiscate: this our censures is.
Lictors proclaime this in the market place,
And see it executed out of hand.

[Exit **LICTOR**.

MARIUS pater
Now see I Senators, the thought, the care,
The vertuous zeale that leads your toward mindes,
To loue your frends and watch your common good:
And now establisht Consull in this place,
Old Marius will foresee aduenient harmes:
Scilla the scourge of Asia as we heare
Is prest to enter Italie with sword,
He comes in pompe to triumph here in Rome,
But Senators you know the wauering wills,
Of foolish men I meane the common sort,
Who through report of innovations,
Or flattering humors of well tempred tongues,
Will change and draw a second mischiefe on:
I like your care, and will my selfe apply
To aime and leuell at my countries weale.
To intercept these errors by aduice,
My sonne yong Marius, Cethegus and my frends,
Shall to Preneste to preuent and stop
The speedie purpose of our forward foe.
Meane while ourselues will fortifie this towne,
This beautie of the world, this maiden towne,
Where streaming Tybris with a pleasant tyde,
Leads out the stately buildings of the world.
Marius my hope, my sonne, you know your charge,
Take those Iberian legions in your traine,
And we will spare some Cymbrians to your vse,
Remember thou art Marius sonne, and dreame
On nought but honor and a happie death.

MARIUS jnr
I go my Lord in hope to make the world
Report my seruice, and my dutie too,
And that proud challenger of Asia,
Shall finde that Marius sonne hath force and wit.

[Exit cum **CETHEGUS**.

MARIUS pater
Goe thou as fortunate as Greekes to Troy
As glorious as Alcides in thy toiles,
As happie as Sertorius in thy fight,
As valiant as A chilles in thy might.
Go glorious, valiant, happie, fortunate,
As all those Greekes and him of Romane state.

[Enter led in with **SOULDIERS**, **CORNELIA** and **FULVIA**.

CORNELIA
Traitors why drag you thus a Princes wife,
As if that beautie were a thrall to fate.
Are Romanes growen more barbarous than Greekes,
That hale more greater than Cassandra now?
The Macedonian Monarch was more kinde,
That honored and relieud in warlike campe
Darius mother, daughters and his wife,
But you unkinde to Romane Ladies now,
Perhaps as constant as the Asian Queenes,
For they subdude had frendship in disgrace,
Where we unconquered liue in wofull case.

MARIUS pater
What plaintiffe pleas presents that Ladie there?
Why souldiers, make you prisners here in Rome?

SOULDIERS
Dread Consulls, we haue found Cornelia here,
And Scillas daughter posting out of towne.

MARIUS pater
Ladies of worth, both beautifull and wise,
But were allied unto my greatest foe:
Yet Marius minde that neuer ment disgrace,
More likes their courage than their comely face.
Are you Cornelia Madame, Scillas wife?

CORNELIA

I am Cornelia Scillas wife: what ther?

MARIUS pater
And is this Fuluia Scillas daughter too?

FULVIA
And this is Fuluia Scillas daughter too.

MARIUS pater
Two welcome guests in whom the maiestie
of my conceit and courage must consist:
What thinke you Senators and countrimen?
See here are two the fairest starres of Rome,
The deerest dainties of my warlike foe,
Whose liues upon your censures do consist.

LEPIDUS
Dread Consull the continuance of their liues,
Shall egge on Scilla to a greater hast.
And in bereauing of their vitall breath,
Your grace shall force more furie from your foe:
Of these extreames we leaue the choice to you.

MARIUS pater
Then thinke that some strange fortune shall insue,

FULVIA
Poore Fulvia, now thy happie daies are done,
In steed of marriage pompe, the fatall lights
Of funeralls must maske about thy bed.
Nor shall thy fathers armes with kinde embrace
Hem in thy shoulders trembling now for feare.
I see in Marius lookes such tragedies,
As feare my hart, and fountaines fills mine eyes.

CORNELIA
Fie Fulvia, shall thy fathers daughter faint
Before the threats of dangers shall approach?
Drie up those teares, and like a Romane maid,
Be bold and silent till our foe haue said.

MARIUS pater
Cornelia wise unto my traitor foe?
What gadding mood hath forst thy speedie slight,
To leaue thy country, and forsake thy frends?

CORNELIA
Accursed Marius, off-spring of my paines,

Whose furious wrath hath wrought thy countries woe:
What may remaine for me or mine in Rome,
That see the tokens of thy tyrannies?
Vile monster, robd of vertue, what reuenge
Is this, to wreake thine anger on the walls?
To race our house, to banish all our frends,
To kill the rest, and captiue vs at last?
Thinkst thou by barbarcos deedes to boast thy state,
Or spoyling Scilla to depresse his hate?
No Marius, but for euerie drop of blood
And inch of wrong he shall returne thee two.

FLACCUS
Madame, in danger wise dome doth aduise,
In humble termes to reconcile our foes.

MARIUS pater
She is a woman Flaccus, let her talke,
That breath forth bitter words in steed of blowes,

CORNELIA
And in regard of that unmodest man,
Thou shouldst desist from outrage and reuenge.

LECTORIUS
What, can your Grace induce these cursed scoffs!

MARIUS pater
Why my Lectorius, I haue euer learnt,
That Ladies cannot wrong me with upbraids.
Then let her talke, and my concealed hate,
Shall heap reuengement upon Scillas pate.

FULVIA
Let feauers first afflict thy feeble age,
Let palsies make thy stubborne fingers faint,
Let humors streaming from thy moystned braines
With cloudes of dymnes choake thy fretfull eyes,
Before these monstrous harmes assaile my syre,

MARIUS pater
By Ladie Fulvia, you are gaily red,
Your mother well may boast you for her owne,
For both of you haue words and scoffs at will:
And since I like the compasse of your wit,
My selfe will stand, and Ladies you shall sit:
And if you please to wade in farther words,
Lets see what brawles your memories affords.

CORNELIA

Your Lordships passing mannerly iniest,
But that you may perceiue we smell your drift,
We both will sit and countenance your shift.

MARIUS pater

Where constancie and beautie doo consort,
There Ladies threatnings turnd to merry sport.
How fare these beautifull, what well at ease?

FULVIA

As readie as at first for to displease.
For full confirmd that we shall surely die,
We wait our ends with Romane constancie.

MARIUS pater

why think you Marius hath confirmd your death!

FULVIA

What other frute may spring from tyrants hands!

MARIUS pater

In faith then Ladies, thus the matter stands,
Since you mistake my loue and curtesie,
Prepare your selues, for you shall surely die.

CORNELIA

I Marius, now I know thou dost not lie:
And that thou maist unto thy lasting blame,
Extinguish in our deaths thy wished fame.
Grant vs this boone that making choice of death,
We may be freed from furie of thine yre,

MARIUS pater

An easie boon, Ladies I condiscend,

CORNELIA

Then suffer vs in priuate chamber close
To meditate a day or two alone:
And tyrant if thou finde vs liuing then,
Commit vs straight unto thy slaughtring men.

MARIUS pater

Ladies I grant, for Marius nill denie,
A sute so easie, and of such import:
For pitie were that Dames of constancie,
Should not be agents of their miserie.

Here he whispers Lectorius.
Lectorius, harke, dispatch.

[Exit **LECTOR**.

CORNELIA
Loe Fulvia, now the latest doome is fixt,
And naught remaines but constant Romane harts,
To beare the brunt of yrksome furies spight,
Rouse thee my deare, and daunt those faint conceipts,
That trembling stand agast at bitter death:
Bethinke thee now that Scilla was thy syre,
Whose courage heauen nor fortune could abate.
Then like the off-spring of fierce Scillas house,
Passe with the thrice renowmed Phrigian Dame,
As to thy marriage, so unto thy death:
For nought to wretches is more sweete than death.

FULVIA
Madam confirmd as well to die as liue,
Fulvia awaiteth nothing but her death.
Yet had my father knowne the course of change,
Or seene our losse by luckie augurie,
Thys tyrant nor hys followers had liued,
To ioy the ruine of fierce Scillas house.

MARIUS pater
But Ladie, they that dwell on fortunes call,
No sooner rise, but subiect are to fall.

FULVIA
Marius I doubt not but our constant endes,
Shall make thee waile thy tyrants gouernment.

MARIUS pater
When tyrants rule doth breed my care & woe
Then will I say two Ladies told me so.
But here comes Lectorius,
Now my Lord, haue you brought those things.

LECTOR
I haue noble Consull.

MARIUS pater
Now Ladies, you are resolute to die.

CORNELIA
I Marius, for terror cannot daunt vs:

Tortors were framde to dread the baser eie,
And not t'appall a princely maiestie.

MARIUS pater
And Marius liues to triumph ore his foes,
That traine where warlike troopes amidst the plaines,
And are inclosde and hemd with shining armes,
Not to apall such princely Maiestie.
Vertue sweete Ladies is of more regard
In Marius minde where honor is inthronde,
Than Rome or rule of Romane Emperie.
Here he puts chaines about their neckes:
The bands that should combine your snow white wrests,
Are these which shall adorne your milke white neckes:
The priuate cells where you shall end your liues,
Is Italy, is Europe, nay the world:
Th'Luxinian sea, and fierce Sicilian Gulph,
The riuer Ganges and Hydaspis streame,
Sha'l leuell lye, and smoothe as christall yce:
Whilst Fuluia and Cornelia passe thereon:
The souldiers that should guard you to your deaths,
Shall be fiue thousand gallant youths of Rome,
In purple roabes crosse bard with pales of gold,
Mounted on warlike coursers for the field,
Fet from the mountaine tops of Cortia,
Or bred in hills of bright Sardinia,
Who shall conduct and bring you to your Lord,
I unto Scilla Ladies shall you goe,
And tell him Marius holds within his hands,
Honor for Ladies, for Ladies rich reward,
But as for Silla and for his compeeres
Who dare gainst Marius vaunt their golden crests,
Tell him for them old Marius holds reuenge,
And in his hands both triumphs life and death.

CORNELIA
Doth Marius vse with glorious words to iest,
And mocke his captiues with these glosing tearmes?

MARIUS pater
No Ladies, Marius hath sought for honour with his sword,
And holds disdaine to triumph in your fals.
Liue Cornelia, liue faire and fairest Fuluia:
If you haue done or wrought me iniurie,
Scilla shall pay it through his miserie.

FULVIA
So gratious (famous Consull) are thy words,

That Rome and we shall celebrate thy worth,
And Scilla shall confesse himselfe orecome.

CORNELIA
If Ladies praiers or teares may mooue the heauens,
Scilla shall vow himselfe old Marius frend.

MARIUS pater
Ladies for that I nought at all regard,
Scilla's my foe, Ile triumph ouer him,
For other conquest glorie doth not win.
Therefore come on, that I may send you unto Scilla,

[Exeunt

[Enter a **CLOWNE** drunke with a pint of wine in his hand, and two or three **SOULDIERS**.

1ST SOULDIER
Sirrha, dally not with us, you know where he is.

CLOWNE
O sir, a quart is a quart in any mans purse, and drinke is drinke, and can my master liue without his drinke I pray you?

2ND SOULDIER
You haue a master then sirrha?

CLOWNE
Haue I master thou scondrell? I haue an Orator to my master, a wise man to my master. But fellowes, I must make a parenthesis of this pint pot, for words make men dry: now by my troth I drinke to Lord Anthonie.

3RD SOULDIER
Fellow souldiers, the weaknes of his braine hath made his tongue walke largely, we shall haue some nouelties by and by.

CLOWNE
Oh most surpassing wine, thou marow of the vine,
More welcome unto me, than whips to schollers bee,
Thou art and euer was a meanes to mend an asse,
Thou makest some to sleep, and manie mo to weep,
And some be glad & merry, with heigh down derry, derry.
Thou makest some to stumble, and many mo to fumble:
And me haue pinkie nine, more braue and iolly wine:
What need I praise thee mo, for thou art good with heigh ho

3RD SOULDIER
If wine then be so good, I pree thee for thy part,

Tell vs where Lord Anthony is, & thou shalt haue a quart.

CLOWNE
First shal the snow be black, & pepper lose his smack
And stripes forsake my backe, first merrie drunke with sack,
I will go boast and tracke, and all your costards cracke,
Before I doo the knacke shall make me sing alacke:
Alacke the old man is wearie, for wine hath made him merrie: with a heigh ho.

1ˢᵀ SOULDIER
I pre thee leaue these rymes, and tell vs where thy master is.

CLOWNE
Faith where you shall not bee vnles ye goe with mee. But shall I tell them so? O no sir, no, no, no, the man hath manie a foe, as farre as I doo know: you doo not flour me I trow. See how this licor fumes, & how my force presumes. You would know where Lord Anthonie is? I perceiue you. Shall I say he is in yond farme house? I deceiue you. Shall I tell you this wine is for him? the gods forfend, and so I end. Go fellow fighters theres a bob for ye.

2ᴺᴰ SOULDIER
My masters, let vs follow this clowne, for questionles this graue orator is in yonder farme house. But who commeth yonder?

[Enter **MARK ANTHONY**.

MARK ANTHONY
I wonder why my peasant staies so long,
And with my wonder hasteth on my woe,
And with my woe I am assaild with feare,
And by my feare await with faintful breath
The final period of my paines by death.

1ˢᵀ SOULDIER
Yonds the man we seeke for (souldiers) vnsheath your swords, and make a riddance of Marius ancient enemie.

CLOWNE
Master flie, flie, or els you shall die: a plague on this wine hath made me so fine, and will you not be gone, then Ile leaue you alone, and sleepe vpon your woe, with a lamentable heigh ho.

[Exit.

MARK ANTHONY
Betraid at last by witles ouersight,
Now Anthony, prepare thy selfe to die:
Loe where the monstrous ministers of wrath
Menace thy murther with their naked swords.

2ND SOULDIER

Anthonie well met, the Consull Marius with other confederate Senators, haue adiudged thee death, therfore prepare thy selfe, and thinke we fauor thee in this little protraction.

MARK ANTHONY

Immortall powers that know the painefull cares,
That waight upon my poore distressed hart,
O bend your browes and leuill all your lookes
Of dreadfull awe upon these daring men.
And thou sweet neece of Atlas on whose lips
And tender tongue, the pliant Muses sit,
Let gentle course of sweet aspiring speech,
Let honnie flowing tearmes of wearie woe,
Let frutefull figures and delightfull lines
Enforce a spring of pitie from their eyes,
Amase the murthrous passions of their mindes,
That they may fauour wofull Anthonie.
Oh countrimen what shal become of Rome,
When reuerend dutie droopeth through disgrace?
Oh Countrimen, what shal become of Rome,
When woful nature widdow of her ioyes,
Weepes on our wals to see her lawes deprest?
Oh Romaines hath not Anthonies discourse,
Seald up the Mouthes of false seditious men,
Assoild the doubts and queint controlls of powre;
Releeud the mournfull matrone with his pleas?
And will you seeke to murder Anthonie?
The Lions brooke with kindnes their releefe,
The sheep reward the shepheard with their fleece:
Yet Romanes seeke to murder Anthony.

1ST SOULDIER

Why what enchanting termes of arte are these?
That force my hart to pitie his distresse.

2ND SOULDIER

His action, speech, his fauor, and his grace,
My rancor rage and rigor doth deface.

3RD SOULDIER

So sweet his words that now of late me seemes
His art doth draw my soule from out my lips.

MARK ANTHONY

What enuious eies reflecting nought but rage,
What barbarous hart refresht with nought but blood,
That rents not to behold the sensles trees
In doaly season drooping without leaues?

The shepheard sighs upon the barrain hills
To see his bleating lambs with faintfull lookes.
Behold the vallies robd of springing flowres,
That whilom wont to yeeld them yerely food.
Euen meanest things exchangd from former state,
The vertuous minde with some remorse doth mate.
Can then your eyes with thundering threats of rage,
Cast furious gleames of anger upon age?
Can then your harts with furies mount so hie,
As they should harme the Romane Anthonie?
I farre more kinde than sensles tree haue lent
A kindly sap to our declining State,
And like a carefull shepheard haue foreseene
The heauie dangers of this Citie Rome,
And made the citizens the happie flocke
Whom I haue fed with counsailes and aduice,
But now those lockes that for their reuerend white,
Surpasse the downe on Aesculapius chin:
But now that tongue whose termes and fluent stile
For number past the hoasts of heauenly fires:
But now that head within whose subtill braines
The Queene of flowring eloquence did dwell:

[Enter a **CAPTAINE**.

These lockes, this tongue, this head, the life and all,
To please a tyrant traitrously must fall.

CAPTAINE
Why how now soldiers is he liuing yet?
And will you be bewitched with his words?
Then take this fee false Orator from me,

[Stab him.

Elizium best beseemes thy faintfull lims.

MARK ANTHONY
Oh blisfull paine, now Anthony must die,
Which serud and loud Rome and her Emperie.

[Moritur.

CAPTAINE
Goe curtall off that necke with present stroke,
And straight present it unto Marius.

1ST SOULDIER

Euen in this head did all the Muses dwell:
The bees that sate upon the Grecians lips,
Distild their honnie on his tempred tongue.

2ND SOULDIER
The christall dew of faire Castalian springs,
With gentle floatings trickled on his braines:
The Graces kist his kinde and curteous browes,
Apollo gaue the beauties of his harpe,

[Enter **LECTORIUS** pensiue.

And melodies unto his pliant speech.

CAPTAINE
Leaue these presumptuous praises, countrimen,
And see Lectorius pensiue where he comes,
Loe here my Lord the head of Anthony,
See here the guerdon fit for Marius foe,
Whom dread Apollo prosper in his rule.

LECTORIUS
Oh Romanes, Marius sleepes among the dead,
And Rome laments the losse of such a frend.

CAPTAINE
A sodaine and a wofull chance my Lord,
Which we intentiue faine would understand.

LECTORIUS
Though swolne with sighs my hart for sorrow burst,
And tongue with teares and plaints be choaked up,
Yet will I furrow forth with forced breath
A speedie passage to my pensiue speech.
Our Consull Marius, worthie souldiers,
Of late within a pleasant plot of ground,
Sate downe for pleasure nere a christall spring,
Accompanied with manie Lords of Rome:
Bright was the day, and on the spredding trees
The frolicke citizens of forrest lung
Their layes and merrie notes on pearching boughes:
When suddenly appeared in the East,
Seauen mightie Eagles with their tallents fierce,
Who wauing oft about our Consulls head,
At last with hideous crie did soare away.
When suddenly old Marius all agast,
With reuerent smile determinde with a sigh
The doubtfull silence of the standers by.

Romanes (said he) old Marius now must die.
These seuen faire Eagles, birds of mightie Ioue,
That at my birth day on my cradle sate,
Now at my last day arme me to my death:
And loe I feele the deadly pangs approach.
What should I more? in briefe, with manie praiers
For Rome, his sonne, his goods and lands disposd,
Our worthie Consull to our wonder dide.
The Citie is amazde, for Scilla hasts
To enter Rome with furie, sword, and fire.
Goe, place that head upon the Capitoll,
And to your wards, for dangers are at hand.

[Exit.

CAPTAINE
Had we foreseene this luckles chance before,
Old Anthonie had liude and breathed yet.

[Exeunt.

ACTUS QUINTAS

SCENA PRIMA

A great skirmish in Rome and long, some slaine. At last enter **SCILLA** triumphant with **POMPEY**,
METELLUS, CITIZENS, SOULDIERS.

SCILLA
Now Romanes after all these mutinies,
Seditions, murthers, and conspiracies,
Imagine with unpartiall harts at last
What frutes proceed from these contentious brawles.
Your streetes, where earst the fathers of your state
In robes of purple walked up and downe,
Are strewd with mangled members, streaming blood.
And why? the reasons of this ruthfull wrack,
Are your seditious innouations,
Your fickle mindes inclinde to foolish change.
Ungratefull men, whilst I with tedious paine
In Asia seald my dutie with my blood,
Making the fierce Dardanians faint for feare,
Spredding my cullers in Galatia,
Dipping my sword in the Enetans blood,
And foraging the fields of Phocida.
You cald my foe from exile with his frends,

You did proclaime me traitor here in Rome,
You racde my house, you did deface my frends,
But brauling wolues, you cannot byte the moone,
For Scilla liues so forward to reuenge,
As woe to those that sought to doo me wrong.
I now am entred Rome in spite of force,
And will so hamper all my cursed foes,
As be he Tribune, Consull, Lord or Knight
That hateth Scilla, let him looke to die.
And first to make an entrance to mine yre,
Bring me that traitor Carbo out of hand.

[Bring in **CARBO** bound.

POMPEY
Oh Scilla, in reuenging iniuries,
Inflict the paine where first offence did spring,
And for my sake establish peace in Rome,
And pardon these repentant Citizens.

SCILLA
Pompey, I loue thee Pompey, and consent
To thy request, but Romanes haue regard,
Least ouer-reaching in offence againe,
I load your shoulders with a double paine.

[Exeunt **CITIZENS**.

But Pompey see where iolly Carbo comes
Footing it featly, like a mightie man,
What no obeisance sirrha to your Lord?
My Lord? No Scilla, he that thrice hath borne
The name of Consull scornes to stoop to him,
Whose hart doth hammer nought but mutinies.

POMPEY
And doth your Lordship then disdaine to stoope

CARBO
I to mine equall Pompey as thou art.

SCILLA
Thine equall villaine, no he is my frend,
Thou but a poore anatomie of bones,
Casde in a knauish tawny withred skin:
Wilt thou not stoop? art thou so stately then?

CARBO

Scilla, I honor gods, not foolish men.

SCILLA
Then bend that wythered bough that will not break
And souldiers cast him downe before my feete:

[They throw him downe.

Now prating sir, my foote upon thy necke,
He be so bold to giue your Lordship checke.
Beleeue me souldiers, but I ouer-reach,
Old Carbos necke at first was made to stretch.

CARBO
Though bodie bend, thou tyrant most unkinde,
Yet neuer shalt thou humble Carbos minde.

SCILLA
oh sir, I know for all your warlike pith,
A man may marre your worship with a wyth.
You sirrha leuied armes to doo me wrong:
You brought your legions to the gates of Rome:
You fought it out in hope that I would faint.
But sirrha now betake you to your bookes,
Intreate the God to saue your sinfull soule.
For why this carcasse must in my behalfe
Goe feast the rauens that serue our augures turne.
Me thinkes I see alreadie how they wish,
To bait their beakes in such a iolly dish.

CARBO
Scilla thy threates and scoffes amate me not:
I pre thee let thy murthrers hale me hence,
For Carbo rather likes to die by sword,
Than liue to be a mocking stocke to thee.

SCILLA
The man hath hast good souldiers take him hence,
It would be good to alter his pretence.
But be aduisde, that when the foole is slaine,
You part the head and bodie both in twaine.
I know that Carbo longs to know the cause,
And shall: thy bodie for the rauens, thy head for dawes.

CARBO
O matchles ruler of our Capitoll,
Behold poore Rome with graue and piteous eie,
Ful-fild with wrong and wretched tyrannie.

[Exit **CARBO** cum militibus.

[Enter **SCIPIO** and **NORBANUS, PUBLIUS LENTULUS**.

SCILLA
Tut the proud mans praier wil neuer pierce the skie.
But whether presse these mincing Senators?

NORBANUS
We presse with praiers, we come with mourn full teares,
Intreating Scilla by those holy bands
That linkes faire Iuno with her thundring Ioue,
Euen by the bounds of hospitalitie,
To pitie Rome afflicted through thy wrath.
Thy souldiers (Scilla) murder innocents.
O whither will thy lawles surie stretch,
If little ruth ensue thy countries harmes.

SCILLA
Gay words Narbonus, full of eloquence,
Accompanied with action and conceipt.
But I must teach thee iudgement therewithall.
Dar'st thou approch my presence that hast borne
Thine armes inspight of Scilla and his frends?
I tell thee foolish man thy iudgement wanted
In this presumptuous purpose that is past:
And loytering scholler, since you faile in art,
Ile learne you iudgement shortly to your smart.
Dispatch him souldiers, I must see him die.
And you Carinna, Carbos ancient frend,
Shall follow straight your heedles Generall.
And Scipio were it not I loud thee well.
Thou shouldst accompanie these slaues to hell:
But get you gone, and if you loue your selfe,

[Exit **SCIPIO**.

CARINNA
Pardon me Scilla, pardon gentle Scilla.

SCILLA
Sirrha, this gentle name was coynd too late,
And shadowed in the shrowds of byting hate.
Dispatch: why so, good fortune to my frends,
As for my foes, euen such shall be their ends.
Conueigh them hence Metellus, gentle Metellus,
Fetch me Sertorius from Iberia,

In dooing so, thou standest me in stead,
For sore I long to see the traitors head.

METELLUS
I goe confirmd to conquer him by sword,
or in th' exployt to hazard life and all.

SCILLA
Now Pompey let me see, those Senators
Are dangerous stops of our pretended state,
And must be curtald least they grow too proud,
I doo proscribe iust fortie Senators,
Which shal be leaders in my tragedie.
And for our Gentlemen are ouer proud,
Of them a thousand and sixe hundreth die,
A goodlie armie meete to conquere hell.
Souldiers performe the course of my decree,
Their friends my foes, their foes shal be my friends,
Go sell their goods by trumpet at your wills,
Meane while Pompey shall see and Rome shall rue,
The miseries that shortly shall ensue.

[Exit.

[Alarum skirmish a retreat, enter young **MARIUS** upon the walles of Preneste with some **SOULDIERS** all in blacke and wonderfull mellancoly.

MARIUS jnr
Oh endles course of needy mans auaile,
What sillie thoughts, what simple pollicies
makes man presume upon this traiterous life?
Haue I not seene the depth of sorrow once,
And then againe haue kist the Queene of chaunce,
Oh Marius thou Tillitius and thy frends,
Hast seene thy foe discomfetted in fight.
But now the starres haue formde my finall harmes,
My father Marius lately dead in Rome,
My foe with honour doth triumph in Rome,
My freends are dead and banished from Rome,
I Marius father freends more blest then thee:
They dead, I liue, I thralled they are free,
Here in Preneste am I cooped up,
Amongst a troope of hunger starved men.
Set to preuent false Scillaes fierce approach.
But now exempted both of life and all.
Well Fortune since thy fleeting change, hath cast
Pore Marius from his hopes and true desiers,
My resolution shall exceed thy power,

Thy coloured wings steeped in purple blood,
Thy blinding wreath distainde in purple blood,
Thy royall Robes washt in my purple blood
Shall witnes to the world thy thirst of blood,
And when the tyrant Scilla shal expect
To see the sonne of Marius stoope for feare,
Then then, Oh then my minde shal well appeare,
That scorne my life and hold mine honour deare.

[Alarum aretreat.

Harke how these murtherous Romaine viperlike,
Seeke to betray their fellow Citizens,
Oh wretched world from whence with speedie slight,
True loue, true zeale, true honour late is fled.

SOULDIER
What makes my Lord so carelesse and secure,
To leaue the breach and here lament alone?

MARIUS jnr
Not feare my frend for I could neuer flie,
But studdy how with honor for to die,
I pray thee cal the cheefest Citizens.
I must aduise them in a waightie cause,
Here shal they meete me and untill they come,
I wil goe view the danger of the breach.

[Exit **MARIUS jnr** and the **SOULDIERS**.

[Enter with drum and **SOULDIERS LUCRETIUS** with other Romanes as **TUDITANUS** &c.

LUCRETIUS
Say Tuditanus, didst thou euer see
So desperate defence as this hath been:

TUDITANUS
As in Numidia Tygers wanting food,
Or as in Libia Lions full of yre,
So fare these Romanes on Preneste wals.

LUCRETIUS
Their valure Tuditanus and resist,
The man like fight of yonger Marius,
Makes me amazd to see their miseries,
And pitie them although they be my foes.
What said I foes? O Rome with ruth I see
Thy state consumde through folly and dissention.

Well sound a parley, I will see if words
Can make them yeeld, which will not flie for strokes?

[Sound a parley, **MARIUS** upon the walls with the **CITIZENS**.

MARIUS
What seeks this Romane warrior at our hands?

LUCRETIUS
That seekes he Marius, that he wisheth thee:
An humble hart, and then a happie peace.
Thou seest thy fortunes are deprest and downe,
Thy vittels spent, thy souldiers weake with want,
The breach laid open readie to assault,
Now since thy meanes and maintenance are done,
Yeeld Marius, yeeld, Prenestians be aduisde,
Lucretius is aduisde to fauor you.
I pre thee Marius marke my last aduice.
Relent in time, let Scilla be thy frend:
So thou in Rome maist lead a happie life,
And those with thee shall pray for Marius still.

MARIUS
Lucretius, I consider on thy words,
Stay there a while thou shalt haue answere straight.

LUCRETIUS
Apollo grant that my perswasions may,
Preserue these Romane souldiers from the sword.

MARIUS
My frends and citizens of Preneste towne,
You see the wayward working of our starres,
Our harts confirmd to fight, our victuals spent.
If we submit, its Scilla must remit,
A tyrant, traitor, enemie to Rome,
Whose hart is guarded still with bloodie thoughts.
These flattring vowes Lucretius here auowes,
Are pleasing words to colour poysoned thoughts.
What will you liue with shame, or die with fame?

1ST CITIZEN
A famous death, my Lord delights vs most.

2ND CITIZEN
We of thy faction (Marius) are resolud
To follow thee in life and death together.

MARIUS
Words full of worth, beseeming noble mindes
The verie Balsamum to mend my woes.
Oh countrimen, you see Campania spoild,
A tyrant threatning mutinies in Rome,
A world dispoyld of vertue, faith and trust.
If then no peace, no libertie, no faith,
Conclude with me, and let it be no life.
Liue not to see your tender infants slaine,
These stately towers made leuell with the land,
This bodie mangled by our enemies sword:
But full resolud to doo as Marius doth,
Unsheath your ponyards, and let euerie frend,
Bethinke him of a souldierlike farewell.
Sirrha, display my standerd on the wals,
And I will answere yond Lucretius,
Who loueth Marius, now must die with Marius.

LUCRETIUS
What answere wil your Lordship then return us?

MARIUS
Lucretius, we that know what Scilla is,
How dissolute, how trothles and corrupt:
In briefe conclude to die before we yeeld:
But so to die (Lucretius marke me well)
As loath to see the furie of our swords
Should murther frends and Romane citizens.
Pie countrimen, what furie doth infect
Your warlike bosomes, that were wont to fight
With forren foes, not with Campanian frends?
Now unaduised youth must counsaile eld:
For gouernance is banisht out of Rome.
Woe to that bough from whence these bloomes are sprung,
Woe to that Aetna, vomiting this fire:
Woe to that brand, consuming Countries weale:
Woe to that Scilla, careles and secure,
That gapes with murther for a Monarchie.
Goe second Brutus with a Romane minde,
And kill that tyrant: and for Marius sake
Pitie the guiltles wiues of these your frends,
Preserue their weeping infants from the sword,
Whose fathers seale their honors with their bloods.
Farewell Lucretius, first I presse in place

[Stab.

To let thee see a constant Romane die,

Prenestians, loe a wound, a fatall wound,
The paine but small, the glorie passing great.

[Againe.

Prenestians see a second stroke: why so.
I feele the dreeping dimnes of the night,
Closing the couerts of my carefull eies.
Follow me frends: for Marius now must die
With fame, in spight of Scillas tyrannie.

[Moritur.

1ST CITIZEN
We follow thee our chiefetaine euen in death,
Our towne is thine Lucretius but we pray
For mercie for our children and our wiues.

[Moritur.

2ND CITIZEN
O saue my forme Lucretius, let him liue,

[Moritur.

LUCRETIUS
A wondrous and bewitched constancie,
Beseeming Marius pride and haughtie minde,
Come let vs charge the breach, the towne is ours
Both male and female put them to the sword:
So please you Scilla, and fulfill his word.

[Exeunt

[A little skirmish, a retreat: enter in royaltie **LUCRETIUS**.

LUCRETIUS
Now Romanes we haue brought Preneste low,
And Marius sleepes amidst the dead at last.
So then to Rome my countrimen with ioy,
Where Scilla waights the tidings of our fight,
Those prisners that are taken, see forth with
With warlike iauelins you put them to death.
Come let vs march, see Rome in sight my harts,
Where Scilla waights the tidings of our warre.

[Enter **SCILLA**, Valerius **FLACCUS: LEPIDUS, POMPEY, CITIZENS GUARD: SCILLA** seated in his robes of
state is saluted by the **CITIZENS**, &c.

FLACCUS
Romanes you know, and to your greefes haue seene
A world of troubles hatched here at home,
Which through preuention being welnigh crost
By worthie Scilla and his warlike band:
I Consull with these fathers thinke it meet
To fortifie our peace and Cities weale,
To name some man of worth that may supply
Dictators power and place, whose maiestie
Shall crosse the courage of rebellious mindes,
What thinke you Romanes, will you condiscend?

SCILLA
Nay Flaccus, for their profits they must yeeld,
For men of meane condition and conceipt
Must humble their opinions to their lords,
And if my frends and Citizens consent
Since I am borne to manage mightie things,
I will (though loth) both rule and gouerne them.
I speake not this as though I wish to raigne,
But for to know my frends: and yet againe
I merrit Romanes farre more grace than this.

FLACCUS
I countrimen, if Scillas powre and mind
If Scillas vertue courage and deuice,
If Scillas frends and fortunes merit fame,
None then but he should beare Dictators name.

POMPEY
What think you Citizens, why stand ye mute?
Shall Scilla be Dictator here in Rome?

CITIZENS
By full consent Scilla shall be Dictator.

FLACCUS
Then in the name of Rome I here present
The rods and axes into Scillas hand,
And fortunate proue Scilla our Dictator.

[Trumpets sound: crie within 'Scilla Dictator'.

SCILLA
My fortunes Flaccus cannot be impeacht,
For at my birth the plannets passing kinde
Could entertaine no retrograde aspects.

And that I may with kindnes quite their loue,
My countrimen I will preuent the cause,
Gainst all the false encounters of mishap.
You name me your Dictator, but prefixe
No time, no course, but giue me leaue to rule,
And yet exempt me not from your reuenge:
Thus by your plesures being set aloft,
Straight by your furies I should quickly fall.
No Citizens, who readeth Scillas minde,
Must forme my titles in another kinde.
Either let Scilla be Dictator euer,
Or flatter Scilla with these titles neuer.

CITIZENS
Perpetuall be thy glorie and renowne,
Perpetuall Lord Dictator shalt thou bee.

POMPEY
Hereto the Senate frankly doth agree.

SCILLA
Then so shall scilla raigne you Senators,
Then so shall Scilla rule you Citizens:
As Senators and Citizens that please mee
Shall be my frends, the rest cannot disease me.

[Enter **LUCRETIUS** with **SOULDIERS**.

But see whereas Lucretius is returnde.
Welcome braue Romaine where is Marius?
Are these Prenestians put unto the sword.

LUCRETIUS
The Cittie noble Scilla raced is,
And Marius dead not by our swords my Lord,
But with more constancie than Cato died,

SCILLA
What constancie and but a verie boy,
Why then I see he was his fathers sonne,
But let vs haue this constancie describde.

LUCRETIUS
After our fearce assaults, and their resist,
Our seige, their salying out to stop our trench:
Labor and hunger rayning in the towne,
The yonger Marius on the Citties wall,
Vouchsafte an interparle at the last:

Wherein with constancie and courrage too,
He boldly armed his freends him selfe to death:
And spreading of his coloures on the wall,
For answere saide he could not brooke to yeeld,
Or trust a tyrant such as Scilla was.

SCILLA
What did the bransicke boy upbraid me so?
But let vs heare the rest Lucretius.

LUCRETIUS
And after great perswsasions to his freends
And worthy resolution of them all:
He first did sheath his ponyard in his breast,
And so in order dyed all the rest.

SCILLA
Now by my sword this was a worthy iest,
Yet silly boy I needs must pittie thee,
Whose noble minde could neuer mated bee,
Beleeue me countrymen a sodaine thought,
A sodaine change in Scilla now hath wrought.
Old Marius and his sonne were men of name,
Nor Fortunes laughes, nor lowers their minds could tame,
And when I count their fortunes that are past,
I see that death confirmde their fames at last.
Then he that striues to manage mightie things,
Amidst his triumphes gaines a troubled minde.
The greatest hope the greater harme it bringes:
And pore men in content their glory finde.
If then content be such a pleasant thing,
Why leaue I country life to liue a king?
Yet Kings are Gods and make the proudest stoope,
Yee but themselues are still pursude with hate
And men were made to mount and then to droope,
Such chances wait upon incertaine fate,
That where she kisseth once shee quelleth twice,
Then who so liues content is happy wise.
What motion moueth this Philosophy?
Oh Scilla see the Ocean ebbs and floats.
The spring-time wanes when winter draweth nie.
I, these are true and most assured notes.
Inconstant chance such tickle turnes hath lent.
As who so feares no fall, must seeke content.

FLACCUS
Whilst grauer thoughts of honor shuld allure thee
What maketh scilla muse and mutter thus?

SCILLA

I that haue past amidst the mightie troopes
Of armed legions through a world of warre,
Doo now bethinke me Flaccus on my chance,
How I alone where manie men were slaine,
In spite of Fate am come to Rome againe,
And so I wield the reuer end stiles of state,
Yea, Scilla with a becke could breake thy necke,
What Lord of Rome hath darde as much as I?
Yet Flaccus knowst thou not that I must die?
The laboring sisters on the weary Loombs,
Haue drawne my webb of life at length, I know:
And men of witt must thinke upon their tombes.
For beasts witt careless steps to Lethe goe:
Where men whose thoughts and honors, clime on hie,
Liuing with fame, must learne, with fame to die.

POMPEY

What lets my Lord in gouerning this state,
To liue in rest, and die with honor too?

SCILLA

What lets me Pompey? why my curteous frend,
Can he remaine secure that weilds a charge?
Or thinke of wit when flattrers doo commend?
Or be aduisde that careles runs at large?
No Pompey, honnie words makes foolish mindes,
And powre the greatest wit with error blindes.
Flaccus, I murdred Anthony thy frend,
Romanes: some here haue lost at my commaund
Their Fathers, Mothers, Brothers, and Allies,
And thinke you Scilla thinking these misdeeds,
Be thinks not on your grudges and mislike?
Yes Countrimen I beare them still in minde.
Then Pompey were I not a silly man,
To leaue my Rule and trust these Romans than?

POMPEY

Your Grace hath small occasions of mistrust,
Nor seeke these Citizens for your disclaime.

SCILLA

But Pompey now these reaching plumes of pride,
That mounted up my fortunes to the Clowds,
By graue conceits shall straight be laid aside,
And scilla thinks of farre more simple shrowds.
For hauing tride occasion in the throne,

Ile see if she dare frowne when state is gone.
Loe senators, the man that sate aloft,
Now deignes to giue inferiors highest place.
Loe here the man whom Rome repined oft,
A priuate man, content to brooke disgrace,
Romanes, loe here the axes, rods and all,
Ile master fortune, least she make me thrall.
Now who so list accuse me, tell my wrongs,
Upbraid me in the presence of this state.
Is none these jolly Citizens among,
That will accuse or say I am ingrate.
Then will I say and boldly boast my chaunces,
That nought may force the man whom Fate aduances.

FLACCUS
What meaneth scilla in this sullen moode,
To leaue his titles on the sodaine thus?

SCILLA
Consull I meane with calme and quiet mind,
To passe my daies while happy death I finde.

POMPEY
What greater wrong, than leaue thy countrey so?

SCILLA
Both it and life must scilla leaue in time.

CITIZEN
Yet during life haue care of Rome and vs.

SCILLA
O wanton world that flatterst in thy prime,
And breathest balme and poyson mixt in one.
See how these wauering Romaines wisht my raigne,
That why lom sought and sought to haue me slaine,
My Countrymen this Cittie wants no store
Of Fathers warriors to supplie my roome,
So grant me peace and I will die for Rome.

[Enter two Burgers to them **POPPEY** and **CURTALL**.

CURTALL
These are verie indiscreet counsailes neighbor Poppey, and I will follow your misaduisement.

POPPEY
I tell you goodman Curtall the wenche hath wrong, oh vaine world, oh foolish men, could a man in nature cast a wench downe, and disdaine in nature to lift her up again? could he take away her

dishonestie without bouncing up the banes of matrimonie? oh learned Poet wel didst thou write Fustian verse.

These maides are dawes that goe to the lawes and a babe in the belly.

CURTALL

Tut man tis the way the world must follow, for maides must be kinde, good husbands to finde.

POPPEY

But marke the fierce if they swell before, it will grieue them sore. but see yondes Master Scilla, faith a prettie fellow is a.

SCILLA

what seekes my countrymen? what would my freendes?

CURTALL

Nay sir your kinde words shall not serue the turne, why thinke you to thrust your souldiers into our kindred with your curtesies sir.

POPPEY

I tel you Master scilla my neighbour wil haue the Law, he had the right he wil haue the wrong for therein dwels the Law.

CONSULL

what desires these men of Rome?

CURTALL

Neighbour sharpen the edge tole of your wits upon the whetstone of indiscretion that your wordes may shaue like the rasers of Palermo, you haue learning with ignorance therefore speake my tale.

POPPEY

Then worshipfull Master Scilla, be it knowne unto you, that my neighbors daughter Doritie was a maid of restoritie, faire fresh and fine as a merrie cup of wine. Her eies like two potcht egges, great and goodly her legs, but marke my dolefull dittie, alas for woe and pittie: a souldier of yours upon a bed of flowers, gaue her such a fall, as she lost maidenhead and all. And thus in verie good time I end my rudefull time.

SCILLA

And what of this my frend, why seeke you mee,
Who haue resignd my titles and my state
To liue a priuate life as you doo now?
Goe moue the Consull Flaccus in this cause,
Who now hath power to execute the lawes.

CURTALL

And are you no more Master dix cator, nor Generalitie of the souldiers?

SCILLA

My powers doo cease, my titles are resignd,

CURTALL

Haue you signd your titles? O base minde, that being in the powles steeple of honor, hast cast thy selfe into the sinke of simplicitie. Fie beast, were I a king, I would day by day sucke up white bread and milke, and go a jetting in a jacket of silke, my meat shou'd be the curds, my drinke should be the whey, and I wold haue a mincing lasse to loue me euerie day.

POPPEY

Nay goodman Curtall, your discretions are verie simple, let me cramp him with a reason. Sirrha, whether is better good ale or small beere? Alas see his implicitie that cannot answere me: why I say ale.

CURTALL

And so say I neighbor.

POPPEY

Thou hast reason, ergo say I tis better be a King than a clowne. Faith master Scilla, I hope a man maye now call ye knaue by authoritie.

SCILLA

With what impatience here I these upbraides
That whilome plagude the least offence with death.
Oh Scilla these are stales of desteny,
By some upbraids to try thy constancie.
My friends these scornes of yours perhaps will moue,
The next Dictator shun to yeeld his state,
For feare he finde as much as Scilla doth.
But Flaccus, to preuent their further wrong,
Vouchsafe some Lictor may attach the man,
And doo them right that thus complaine abuse.

FLACCUS

Sirrha, goe you and bring the souldier
That hath so loosly leant to lawles lust,
We will haue meanes sufficient be assurd
To coole his heate, and make the wanton chast.

CURTALL

We thanke your mastership: come neighbour, let vs iog, faith this newes will set my daughter Dorothie a gog.

[Exeunt cum **LICTORE**.

SCILLA

Graue Senators and Romanes, now you see
The humble bent of Scillas changed minde.
Now will I leaue you Lords, from courtly traine
To dwel content amidst my country caue,
Where no ambitious humors shall approach,
The quiet silence of my happy sleepe.

Where no delicious louisance or toyes,
Shall tickle with delight my tempered eares,
But wearying out the lingering day with toile,
Tyring my veines and furrowing of my soule.
The silent night with slumber stealing on
Shall locke these carefull closets of mine eies.
Oh had I knowne the height of happines,
Or bent mine eies upon my mother earth:
Long since O Rome had Scilla with reioyce
Forsaken armes to leade a priuate life.

FLACCUS

But in this humblenes of minde my Lord,
Whereas experience prooude and Art doo meete.
How happy were these faire Italian fields,
If they were graced with so sweete a sunne:
Then I for Rome and Rome with me requires,
That Scilla will abide and gouerne Rome.

SCILLA

O Flaccus, if th'Arabian Phoenix striue
By natures warning to renue her kinde,
When soaring nie the glorious eye of heauen,
Shee from her cinders doth reuiue her sexe.
Why should not Scilla learne by her to die?
That carst haue beene the Phoenix of this land.
And drawing neere the sunne-shine of content,
Perish obscure to make your glories growe.
For as the higher trees do shield the shrubs,
From posting Phlegons warmth and breathing fire,
So mighty men obscure each others fame,
And make the best deseruers fortunes game.

[Enter **GENIUS**.

But ah what sodaine furies do affright?
What apparitious fantasies are these?
Oh let me rest sweete Lords, for why me thinks,
Some fatall spells are sounded in mine eares.

GENIUS

Subsequitur tua moors: priuari lumine Scillam,
Numina Parcarum iam fera precipiunt.
Precipiunt fera iam Parcarum numina, Scillam,
Lumine priuari, mors tua subsequitur,
Elysium petis, ô foelix! & fatidici astri:
Praescius Heroas, ô petis innumeros!
Innumeros petis ô Heroas! praescius astri

Fatidici: & foelix, ô petis Elisium!
Euanescit subitò.

SCILLA
Ergóne post dulces annos properantia fata?
Ergóne iam tenebrae pramia lucis erunt?
Attamen, vt vitae fortunam gloria mortis
Vincat, in extremo funere cantet olor.

POMPEY
How fares my Lord? what dreadful thoughts are these
What doubtfull answeres on a sodaine thus?

SCILLA
Pompey the man that made the world to stoope,
And fettered fortune in the chaines of powre,
Must droope and draw the Chariot of Fate
Along the darksome bankes of Acheron.
The heauens haue warnd me of my present fall.
Oh call Cornelia forth, let Scilla see
His daughter Fuluia ere his eyes be shut.

[Exit one for **CORNELIA**.

FLACCUS
Why Scilla, where is now thy wonted hope
In greatest hazard of unstaied chance?
What shall a little biting blast of paine
Blemish the blossomes of thy wonted pride?

SCILLA
My Flaccus, worldly ioyes and pleasures fade,
In constant time like to the fleeting tide
With endles course mans hopes doth ouer-beare?
Nought now remaines that Scilla faine would haue,
But lasting fame when bodie lies in graue.

[Enter **CORNELIA, FULVIA**.

CORNELIA
How fares my Lord? how doth my gentle Scilla?

SCILLA
Ah my Cornelia passing happie now.
Free from the world, allied unto the heauens,
Not curious of incertaine chaunces now.

CORNELIA

Words full of woe still adding to my griefe,
A curelesse crosse of many hundreth harmes.
Oh let not Rome and poore Cornelia loose,
The one her frend, the other her delight.

SCILLA
Cornelia, man hath power by some instinct
And gracious reuolution of the starres,
To conquer kingdomes not to master fate:
For when the course of mortall life is runne,
Then Clotho ends the web hir sister spun.
Pompey, Lord Flaccus, fellow senators,
In that I feele the faintfull deawes of death
steeping mine eies within their chilly wet,
The care I haue of wife and daughter both,
Must on your wisedomes happily relie,
With equall distribution see you part,
My lands and goods betwixt these louely twaine,
Onely bestow a hundred thousand Sestercies,
Upon my friends and fellow souldiers.
Thus hauing made my finall testament,
Come Fuluia let thy father lay his hand,
Upon thy louely bosome and intreat
A vertuous boone and fauour at thy hands.
Faire Romane maide, see that thou wed thy faires,
To modest vertuous and delightfull thoughts:
Let Rome in viewing thee behold thy sire,
Honour Cornelia from whose fruitfull woombe,
Thy plenteous beauties sweetly did appeare,
And with this Lesson louely maide farewell.

FULVIA
Oh tedious and unhappy chance for me.

SCILLA
Content thee Fuluia, for it needes must bee.
Cornelia I must leaue thee to the world,
And by those loues that I haue lent thee oft,
In mutuall wedlocke rytes and happie warre.
Remember Scilla in my Fuluia stil:
Consull farewell, my Pompey I must hence,
And farewel Rome, and Fortune now I blesse thee,
That both in life and death wouldst not oppresse mee,

[Dies.

CORNELIA
Oh hideous stormes of neuer danted fate,

Now are those eyes whose sweet reflections coold
The smothered rancors of rebellious thoughts
Clad with the sable mantles of the night.
And like the tree that robd of sunne and showres
Mournes desolate withouten leafe or sap:
so poore Cornelia late bereft of love,
Sits sighing, haples, ioyles and forlorne.

FULVIA
Gone is the flower that did adorne our fields,
Fled are those sweete reflections of delight,
Dead is my Father, Fuluia dead is hee
In whom thy life, for whom thy death must bee.

FLACCUS
Ladies, to tyre the time in restles mone
Were tedious unto frends and nature too,
Sufficeth you that Scilla so is dead,
As fame shall sing his power though life be fled.

POMPEY
Then to conclude his happines my Lords,
Determine where shall be his Funerall.

LEPIDUS
Euen there where other Nobles are interd.

POMPEY
Why Lepidus what Romane euer was,
That merited so high a name as hee?
Then why with simple pompe and funerall
Would you intombe so rare a paragon?

CORNELIA
An urne of gold shall hem his ashes in,
The Vestall virgins with their holy notes
Shall sing his famous (though too fatall) death,
I and my Fuluia with dispersed haire
Will waight upon this noble Romanes hearse.

FULVIA
And Fuluia clad in blacke & mournfull pale
Will waight upon her fathers funerall.

POMPEY
Come beare we hence this trophee of renowne,
Whose life, whose death was farre from fortunes frowne,

[Exeunt **OMNES**.

The Funeralls of Scilla in great pompe.
Deo iuuante, nil nocet liuor malus:
Et non iuuante nil iuuat labor grauis.

FINIS.

THOMAS LODGE – A CONCISE BIBLIOGRAPHY

c1580 Defence of Plays
1584 An Alarum against Usurers
1589 Scillaes Metamorphysis (reprinted in 1610 as A most pleasant Historie of Glaucus and Scilla)
1590 Rosalynde
1591 Robert, Second Duke of Normandy
1591 Catharos
1592 Euphues Shadow
1593 Phillis
1593 William Longbeard
1594 The Wounds of Civill War
1594 A Looking Glass for London (in collaboration with Robert Greene)
1595 A Fig for Momus
1596 The Divel coniured
1596 A Margarite of America
1596 Wits miserie
1596 Prosopopeia
1602 Paradoxes
1602 Works of Josephus
1603 A Treatise of the Plague
1614 The Workes of Seneca
1625 A Learned Summary of Du Bartas

www.ingramcontent.com/pod-product-compliance
Lightning Source LLC
Chambersburg PA
CBHW060142050426
42448CB00010B/2254